Who's That Woman in the Mirror?

Who's that Woman in the Mirror?

Keren Smedley

Illustrations by Stephen Garrett

headline
springboard

First published in 2008
by HEADLINE SPRINGBOARD

An imprint of Headline Publishing Group

1

Cataloguing in Publication Data is available from the British Library.

978 0 7553 1756 1

Typeset in Times by Palimpsest Book Production Ltd, Grangemouth, Stirlingshire

Printed and bound in Great Britain by Mackays of Chatham plc, Chatham, Kent

Headline's policy is to use papers that are natural, renewable and recyclable products
and made from wood grown in sustainable forests.
The logging and manufacturing processes are expected to conform to the
environmental regulations of the country of origin.

HEADLINE PUBLISHING GROUP
An Hachette Livre UK Company
338 Euston Road
London NW1 3BH

www.headline.co.uk

www.hachettelivre.co.uk

To Martin, Ben, Timmy, Matthew and my mother, who have taught me how to age – and how not to.

Acknowledgements

Special thanks to Richard Barber, without whom the words wouldn't flow; Kathleen Reddington for her infinite support, ideas and help with every aspect; Jacky Spigel for her insider knowledge; Stephen Garrett for his great cartoons and getting into the mind of the 50+; and Martin Gelgyn for numerous meals to sustain me.

Thanks, too, to Patti Barber, Denise Blake, Sue de Botton, Daphne Carnegy, Karen Cohen, Barbara Elton, Chris Kell, Margy Knutson, Andrea Stern, Sue Temple, Helen Whitten and Jane Williamson for talking to me about being 50+ and sharing their ideas on what women need.

Also, to Rosie Scourti for her help with research; Ben Smedley for his professional input; Ashley Meyers and Ranjana Appoo for their knowledge of EFT; and my many clients for all their questions and shared thoughts.

Finally, to my agent, Amanda Preston, who believed in the book from the start and encouraged me all the way; and Val Hudson at Headline, who saw the potential and ultimately made it happen; Jane Butcher for her copy-editing; and Philippa Hobbs and Helena Towers for their support.

Contents

Section Two
You're Never Too Old to ... Look Good

Section Four
You're Never Too Old to ... Juggle Life   127

Introduction

'You can't help getting older but you don't have to get old.'
George Burns

All this talk of 50 being the new 30, and 60 the new 40, may make catchpenny newspaper headlines, but it doesn't amount to a hill of beans. For baby boomers now staring 50 or 60 in the face, the issues raised are far more complex as a new generation journeys into the unknown.

Because not only will the face staring back at you from the bathroom mirror look years younger than your grandparents did at the same age, but the potential anxieties of older age today are infinitely more complicated – and quite different – from the so-called retirement previous generations accepted as their inevitable fate.

I've worked now for over twenty years as a coach, consultant and counsellor. As a baby boomer myself, I have reached a 'certain age' but am still full of energy and innovative ideas. I find that many of my 50+ clients are regularly raising issues in coaching sessions which are related to age. As a specialist in organisational and people development, I have both the life skills and expertise to help others to challenge these issues and to find new and interesting ways to manage their lives. So I set up Experience Matters Limited, a company that specialises in coaching and consulting on age-related issues, to help individuals and organisations to find positive solutions. As Saga's (an organisation dedicated to the 50+) life coach, I answer readers' personal questions on the Saga website. I feel passionate about altering outdated stereotypes about age and helping people to change their beliefs and attitudes so that this period of their life is as productive and fruitful as the last.

Spool back two or three generations and the Bible's assumption of a life expectancy that would encompass no more than 'three score years and ten' proved pretty accurate. But that was then. Now, the women (and some men, too) whom I meet in my work know full well that, unless they're unlucky, they could live twenty or thirty years beyond the traditional retirement age. And it can frighten them silly.

Naturally, not all 50- to 60-year-olds are the same, far from it. We all have life stories that are different with different influences and experiences. These of course affect our attitudes to age. So, how do you manage, how do you plan ahead for two decades and more after you've stopped working? Do you stop working? How do you pace yourself? How do you juggle your finances? How do we stay vibrant and sexy well beyond the days our mothers dared think about sex? With no blueprint of a previous generation's experience on which to draw, it can seem a bewildering prospect.

The feminist movement was far from perfect. It did encourage young women in the sixties and seventies, though, to express their innermost feelings to their contemporaries. But ask most women today who've cleared the hurdle of their fiftieth birthday and they'll tell you that, at most, they might have only two or three female confidantes. I know: my 'surgery' is full of them.

Since the same questions and insecurities – over looks, love, loss, the problems of dealing with adult children and increasingly elderly parents – are raised time and time again in my conversations with individual clients, I have arranged this book into six sections. Each section will deal with a distinct topic, specifically answering a set of oft-repeated anxieties. Exercises and questionnaires are included that will enable the reader to assess what action could be taken next.

There is, of course, no blanket answer to any of the challenges posed by entering what romantic novelists call the 'autumn of your life'. But, if this book can at least point you in the right direction as you adjust to the unfamiliar concept of having so much more time on your hands and, if it can help you regard that prospect with a sense of wonder and curiosity rather than an imminent panic attack, then its compilation won't have been in vain.

As to age itself . . . phooey! Joan Collins, that byword for timeless glamour, is a major disciple of George Burns's maxim. I once read somewhere a quote of hers that I'll never forget, 'Age is irrelevant,' she said, 'unless you happen to be a bottle of wine.'

Couldn't have put it better myself.

✖ Section One ✖

You're Never Too Old to...
Dream the Impossible
Dream

Dreaming is something all of us will have done since we were very young when we played make-believe. Most of us will have moments when we find ourselves somewhere else: we get caught up in a daydream. However, sometimes when we ask older people to talk about their daydreams, they reply, 'I'm too old to do that.' Other people will tell you they're too scared to dream because their lives are going through a bad patch and they don't believe good things are possible. Still others believe they're living the dream and never take a realistic view as to where they are and what is possible. A happy medium is the answer, which is, of course, true for most things.

We have grown up in an age of positive thinking (more on that in Question 3 in this section and Section 6, Question 2) and with the idea that having clear goals is the route to success, even though life may not be quite like the Everly Brothers' song 'All I Have to Do Is Dream'. Having a dream or goal is pretty essential if you're going to achieve what you want. Highly successful people will tell you that having a dream or goal at the forefront of their mind is what got them to where they are today.

This section's questions focus on goals and dreams.

Q1 **I am nearing retirement. I see my life as a bit of a blank in front of me. I always thought I'd know what I wanted to do with my life by now, but I just don't seem able to crystallise my thoughts. How do I do this? I don't want to waste these years.**

The idea of retirement is one that all of us baby boomers have grown up working towards, believing that, if we're fortunate enough to be healthy and make it to our sixties, life will be for the taking. But retirement has so many connotations. Early voluntary retirement sounds like fun (if you have the resources to finance it), but retirement because you've reached an age synonymous with being 'old' is not that appealing!

For those of you interested in history, the idea of a fixed retirement age is of recent origin. It was introduced during the nineteenth and twentieth centuries; the earliest system was developed in Germany in 1889. In the UK, a universal state pension was first introduced in 1948. Prior to this, the lack of pension arrangements meant that most people continued to work until they died.

I wonder from your question if one of the things stopping you from seeing your future is your negative feelings about retirement itself. When you imagine a retired person, what is the first picture that comes to mind? Is it a fit 55-year-old trekking across the Himalayas with a rucksack on their back? Or a person of 65 actively pursuing new hobbies and interests? Or is it perhaps an old person, probably twenty to thirty years older than you, worn down and wearing carpet slippers?

For you, retirement is just around the corner. If, whenever we contemplate retirement, we immediately associate it with old age – something that hasn't as yet had a very good press – it must appear a fairly unappealing prospect. No wonder you have a blank when you think about it. It never ceases to amaze me just how protective our unconscious minds can be: a blank rather than a more difficult picture. The thing is, as you obviously know from your question, a blank isn't going to get you very far in planning and taking control of your life. As Richard Bandler suggests in his book *Using Your Brain for a Change*, who runs your head? Whose head is it anyway? We have a choice as to what we put into our heads – good or bad. That is such an empowering thought. All we need to do is learn how to control the thoughts and images we walk around with and we can have so much better and easier a time. Work at putting great pictures in there rather than blanks or horror images.

As with everything you learn, new skills take time and practice. If you're someone who finds creating positive images pretty easy, then fine, but, if changing your outlook poses problems, it'll be a bit of a stretch. (See Section 5, Question 1 on thinking preferences.) But, believe me (and I am one of the latter), with practise you can make it work. The following exercise will get you started.

EXERCISE: FUTURE PERFECT

Find a place where you can have a bit of space, peace and quiet, somewhere you'll be free to think. Take a notepad and pen with you.

1. Imagine your life-line in front of you – in other words, a line that goes from when you were born till you're 90 or 100. We're going to work in ten-year cycles so you can have it, quite literally, laid out in front of you.

2. Stand at the end of the first stretch, 0–10 years. You may well not remember much in this period, but you will remember the significant bits – going to school, the arrival of a new sibling, moving house and so on. Write it all down. In your mind, walk along your line slowly, remembering all the things that happened to you. Just allow your thoughts to flow freely. It doesn't matter how much or how little you recall. When you get to 10, fold up that bit of the paper and start again with 11–20. Continue doing this until you get to today; let's say 64.

3. Now put 64 at the start and go to the far end of your line where you've reached 94. Imagine yourself at 94 looking back over the last 30 years. What have you been doing? How have you filled your time? Is there anything missing? Put in all the things you have ever wanted to do. Is your list full of chores or full of fun? What are the things you've always wanted to do but not had the time? Make sure all of these are included, too. Don't just put what is possible but also what you really want.

4. Go back to your line and walk from 64 to 94 through all those desires. Keep an eye on the list to make sure you haven't missed anything out.

5. As you walked along the line, did any particular timings come to you – for example, I must move house by the time I'm 70? Again, jot down your dates. You'll now have a broad overview of what you want to do.

6. Put your piece of paper away and just let your head sort out the planning while you get on with other things. If any other ideas come to mind, then jot them down.

7. In a week or so, take a look at your list – what do you think? Your immediate reaction may be, 'I can't do that' or 'That's a mad idea' or 'My children/partner/friends would be appalled.' If any of these have been your reaction, go to Section 4, Question 1 on critical voices.

Imagine that there are no barriers, physical or emotional, and it's all just down to your choice. There may be things that no longer appeal. If so, cross them out. Also, add in any last-minute ambitions. If you do this, you will certainly have achieved your desire to crystallise your thoughts and know what you want.

If, at any stage, negative thoughts reoccur, get out your line and recreate your dream. We all know when we get to this age that life cannot simply be lived along a linear line. The unexpected and unwanted do happen so modifications may need to be made.

The next question articulates additional, understandable anxieties.

Q2 **I find myself worrying about my life. I work full time at the moment. I am coming up to 60 and know that I really have to do the things I want to do before it is too late. I just don't know how to go about it. What can I do?**

It seems to me there are two issues here. One is to do with worry. Are you someone who worries all the time about everything and, in this instance, have you linked your worrying to being 60? I discuss worrying in Section 6, Question 5. For now, let's focus on the other issue: how to get what you want.

However, before we do, let's just address the magic number of 60. Reaching that age seems to give most of us (even non-habitual worriers) licence to be concerned about our impending old age. It's a time – or so many of us imagine – when things begin to fall apart, a time when you officially move from middle age to old age. As the timelessly youthful Doris Day once said, 'The really frightening thing about middle age is that you know you'll grow out of it!'

The state pension age for women is changing – it will rise gradually from age 60 to 65 between 2010 and 2020. From 6 April 2020, the state pension age for both men and women will be 65. The pension service at www.thepensionservice.gov.uk has a calculator which will work out the date of your retirement for you instantly.

As yet, the age we all qualify for a free travel pass or concessionary pass remains 60, but there's no guarantee that that's set in stone. Before long, 60 could well become no more than another birthday with a nought in it. Our children won't notice being 60 any more than any of the other big birthdays. It will be a different age for them that comes to mean old – 70, 80, even 90!

The one thing that *is* true is that we are all getting older. But even if we have thirty years or more to enjoy ourselves and do interesting things, we've obviously got less time than we did when we were young. You say you know what you want but are stuck on how to get there. You also say that you're working full time, which probably means you have little time to spare.

A common way of preventing ourselves from succeeding is to set unrealistic expectations. If we set ourselves goals or have a vision that is not achievable, we're always going to be disappointed. Let's imagine for a minute that you've been invited to a party by a friend. You're really looking forward to dancing the evening away as this friend always plays good music. You arrive and find it's a dinner party not a dance party at all. Your vision doesn't meet reality and you're disappointed, even though the food is great and so is the company.

If we reverse this now and you imagine a second invite to a party from someone you find pretty dull, you feel you ought to go but your expectation is that it will be boring and you'll be home by ten. When you arrive, you bump straight into an old friend you haven't seen for years and spend the evening talking to her and other old friends and you don't get to bed till well after midnight. You will have exceeded your expectations and will feel very good. It's all to do with Vision versus Reality:

$$\text{If } V=R, \text{ we're doing OK}$$
$$\text{If } V>R, \text{ we're disappointed}$$
$$\text{If } V<R, \text{ we feel good}$$

EXERCISE: ACTION PLANNING

I. Take a piece of A4 paper and write down a list of all the things that you want to do/achieve.

2. Why are they important to you?

3. Which three are the most important to you?

4. Let's concentrate on those three. Now, beside each of them, write down how you'll know you've achieved your ambition. For example, don't write, 'I want to be thinner.' Write, 'I want to be able to wear clothes one size smaller.'

5. Now write down the date by which you want to have achieved this goal.

6. Imagine that a friend of yours has handed you this list. How realistic is it? Have you put too many items down to be completed in a very short time?

You may like to use the time wheel diagram to easily visualise how you spend your time.

Time Wheel

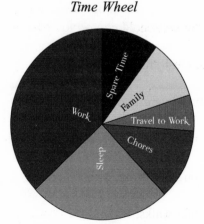

Write down all the things you have to do in one week. Work out approximately how long you spend on each. For example:

Jane works full time. She has wanted to learn a new language as she plans to travel more when she is working less. She is fed up with herself because, in spite of her goal, she never seems to manage to attend the language classes regularly. When asked to write down what she had done during her week, Jane wrote:

Mon to Fri: each day 8 hours of work, 2 hours of household chores, 8 hours' sleep – so 6 hours for relaxation and other activities.
Sat and Sun: 9 hours' sleep, 3 hours of household chores – so 12 hours for free time each day.
That's 54 hours of free time each week.

She was amazed, as it didn't feel like that. She seems to be busy all of the time. I then asked Jane a number of questions:

● Who do you spend time with during the week?

  She mentioned her mother, her partner, her two school-aged children and her brother.

● What are the household chores you have to do?

  Shop, iron, clean, mend, garden.

● What hobbies/interests do you have?

  She listed music, cinema, reading and theatre.

● What do you do to relax?

  She likes long walks, watching TV and meeting friends.

None of these were in her original list, let alone all the ordinary activities we take for granted such as getting washed and dressed.

Looking at this more closely, Jane spends approximately 1 hour a day getting washed and dressed, 1 hour a day preparing and eating meals, 1 hour a day talking to her family and friends on the phone, 4 hours a week helping her children do their homework, 3 hours a week being their chauffeur, 3 hours on both weekend days visiting her elderly mother and 1 hour twice a week checking on carers, talking to her brother about her mother and so on. That all adds up to 36 hours a week so all she has left when you deduct this time is 18 hours for all the other things she wants to do.

Once Jane was aware of how she spent her time, she stopped berating herself and realised that, if she really wanted to learn a language, something else would have to give. This realisation had quite an effect on Jane and she made some significant changes to the way she spent her week so she could give 5 hours to learning another language.

Having worked out your week, you now have a realistic idea of how much time you have at your disposal. Ask yourself the following questions: what is the first step I need to take? And by when? How will I celebrate when I have achieved this? What will my next step be?

Unrealistic goals are, of course, not the only reasons for not getting things done. There are other reasons, such as feeling bad about yourself, which is self-sabotage (see Section 3, Question 1) and a lack of self-confidence (see Section 5, Question 4).

Q3 **I feel sad that I've got to this stage in my life and there are things I know I'll never do because I'm too old, e.g. be a ballerina or a brain surgeon. I also find it hard to hold on to what I've already achieved. I'm prone**

to depression and find that these thoughts of what I've missed are with me too much of the time. What can I do?

From what you've told me, it seems you're a glass-half-empty rather than a glass-half-full person. What's really important is how not to let missed opportunities cloud the good feelings you should be experiencing about your life, how not to dwell on the negative. Personally, I believe there's a place for both outlooks.

I find the 'always positive' brigade, when faced even with a tragedy in someone's life, hard to stomach. Equally, always dwelling on the negative is bound to have a debilitating effect. So we have to learn to re-frame things and see them from a number of different angles and then move on. Find a way to remember your past and the pleasure it has given you and use this to find the energy to move into the future.

Give the following exercise a go.

EXERCISE: REMEMBER YOUR PAST (ASSOCIATION TECHNIQUE)

1. Find a quiet place to sit. If we're going to help ourselves to find a more fulfilling life, we need time and space to think. Sometimes, you can find thinking time while doing other things like gardening or travelling. Next time you're on a train or bus or plane keep your book or magazine in your bag and just think; or while you're having a long hot soak in the bath or even while you're doing a mind-numbing domestic chore like ironing. Learning to think usefully is a knack anyone can acquire.

2. So, having found your thinking place, spool back in
   your mind to a time when you felt really happy and
   were having a good time – like going out for a meal
   with friends, going for a walk somewhere beautiful,
   watching your child swim their first width. It really
   doesn't matter what it is. As you imagine it, create a
   picture of this event. Are you in the picture or outside
   it? Are you looking at it as though you're watching it
   on television, or are you there feeling it, seeing it,
   smelling it, tasting it? Just jot down whether you're in
   or out of your picture.

3. Now think of something that made you feel a bit fed up,
   like your car having a puncture, or your boss being in a bad
   mood, or a friend cancelling a dinner date. Create a picture
   of this event. Are you in it or out of it? Again just note it
   down.

4. Now recreate your happy picture. This time, I want you
   to climb into it. When you are back reliving an
   experience, you are associated with it; and when you are
   observing the event, you are disassociated. See what you
   see, hear what you hear, feel what you feel. Take yourself
   back there and make it your present. Note what is
   happening to you. How are you feeling? As you do this,
   re-associate with the good experiences, relive them.
   Your body will respond physiologically and the 'feel
   good' chemicals such as serotonin will flow into your
   body. Do this exercise every day for a month and really
   learn to enjoy yourself and value what you've
   experienced.

5. Now go back to your negative experience just for a
   minute. Climb back in there. Relive what happened –
   yep, you feel bad! Not a sensible thing to do, I know, so

climb straight out and get back into the happy picture. I know things go wrong and we can have some pretty difficult times. However, reliving these experiences is a sure-fire way of being miserable and won't solve anything. We need to be able to find a way to deal with them and move on.

EXERCISE: THINK POSITIVE

1. Think of something that is happening which is not going the way you want and it feels difficult. Create this picture and imagine it painted on the wall.

2. Take a look at it. What are the people involved doing? What would you advise the 'you' in that picture to be doing? Tell her what needs to be done.

3. Write down how she could improve the situation and keep this as a crib sheet when you're next involved in a similarly difficult situation.

The trick, when dealing with difficult situations, is to remove ourselves emotionally and then, nine times out of ten, the solution will present itself. Associating into positive experiences and disassociating from negative ones enables us to enjoy the benefits and learn from our mistakes.

You say you are prone to depression. Sometimes we find ourselves stuck for someone else to talk to. If there is no particular friend in whom you can confide, consider going to a GP or a therapist/counsellor. Clearly, you can't go back and relive your past all over again but it is possible to revisit it and extract from it only the good bits.

Q4 **I'm 54 years old. My friends are talking about their retirement and what they're going to do – carry on working, travel the world, start some amazing new job, write a bestseller or end up penniless and dependent on their children or the state. All the time they're talking, I'm screaming inside. Having survived breast cancer four years ago, I worry whether I'll make it to 60. How do I, first, cope with these feelings and, second, tell my friends I find it hard, without sounding negative or depressing?**

There's no denying it: it's tough. We tend to assume we'll live to a great old age as life expectancy is increasing. What's more, there have been no world wars for over sixty years.

However, we all know that's not how it will be for everyone. By the time you're into your fifties, you'll almost certainly know of acquaintances, friends or family who've died before their 'three score years and ten'. And anyone over 50 will have experienced how their body has changed and is not functioning as well as it once did. We'll all have had moments when we're aware of our own physical frailty with a limited time span. The fact that no one worried about our blood pressure or cholesterol when we were 20 years younger is further proof of this.

The baby boomers in the main are an optimistic group. This was the legacy they inherited from their parents, who lived through very different, more difficult times and who wanted their children to reap the benefits of a secure post-war era. We tend to focus on the positives in life. We often appear publicly as though we are in denial of our ageing bodies, our health issues and our own mortality. You've had to deal with a real and serious health issue. You've been through a very rough time and it would be odd if it hadn't made you sad and scared. So it's not surprising you feel as you do.

You pose two really important questions. Let's start with you and your feelings and then move on to your friends. My hunch is that, once you understand what's happening with your emotions and start to feel more at ease with yourself, you'll find it easier to manage your pals. Recent evidence has shown that dwelling on our negative feelings has a detrimental effect on our health.

Elisabeth Kübler-Ross, a Swiss-born psychiatrist, revolutionised doctors' approach to grief and bereavement in the terminally ill. She wrote a seminal book in 1969, *On Death and Dying*, where she explains both her five-stage grief model, i.e. the processes people go through (denial, anger, bargaining, depression and acceptance), and how to support people through the grief process. Her work is still a basic text for all medical and social-work students and her ideas are transferable to personal change and emotional upset due to factors other than death or dying.

Faced with a diagnosis of cancer or another serious illness, some people will hear it as a death sentence. However many reassurances given at the point of diagnosis, their immediate reaction will be that they're dying. Others will go into denial and not hear what they're being told and certainly not believe it. Some will become hysterical and either laugh it off or become seriously depressed. A further number will vow to fight this by themselves without any need of medical intervention. We all do the best we can at that moment and, although our reactions may not suit others, they are our way of protecting ourselves. It is important that others honour this and don't push us to listen to their suggestions until we have had time to take in the shocking information.

The diagram based on Elisabeth Kübler-Ross's grief cycle shows the process people typically follow:

Grief Cycle

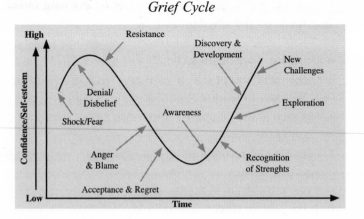

When we're presented with horrible or difficult news, we usually experience the following arc of emotions:

- Shock – resulting from a 'disconnection' between the new situation and our existing understanding and beliefs about reality. We hear ourselves saying, 'It's not possible.'

- Denial – the information/new situation is mentally resisted. Sometimes, people just carry on as if nothing has happened or they become more energetic and active. It's as if they need to fight and prove they're invincible and can manage the situation by themselves.

- Resistance – this phase may continue for a while with reality being resisted by holding on to our original beliefs as strongly as we know how – by repeating, for example, 'I am a very healthy person and I don't get ill.'

- Anger and blame – the deep fear that is felt by anyone in this situation often manifests itself in anger and blame rather than on what's happening. Both can be internally and/or externally focused. We blame ourselves, our family, our genes, our doctors, anyone or anything rather than focus on the situation as it is.

- Acceptance – we begin to be able to process what has happened and accept that we are not our normal healthy self. We start to work out how to manage things. This acceptance is the beginning of the more positive phases.

- Awareness and recognition of our strengths – we begin to realise that we can do something about what's happening and our self-esteem starts to reassert itself. We often surprise ourselves with our ability to cope. We do this through re-evaluating ourselves and our lives in relation to the new, now accepted situation.

- Exploration – we now have some energy available to explore possibilities rather than impossibilities and to make some choices.

- Discovery – we find a new way to do things, new meanings in our lives. We develop an understanding which can both deepen existing relationships and foster new ones. We interweave these new experiences with existing ones and become more at peace with how we are.

- New challenges – as a result of this new awareness, we feel more positive and are able to contemplate a viable future. There are many instances of people undertaking exciting new activities they never expected to tackle. They stop waiting for something that might or might not happen and start getting on with their lives.

This is a generalised process and the way we take ourselves through it will, of course, be different for everyone. We move at our own pace, sticking at one bit or another and going backwards as well as forwards. There are some people who get more or less permanently stuck at a particular stage and never appear to move on. A typical example would be someone who remains angry that a loved one has died and the anger becomes part of who they are.

Whenever anyone mentions anything to you that triggers your grief memory, it will jump you back into the old cycle. You'll feel as if you're there, reliving the painful diagnosis and it will be powerful enough to hurt you all over again. (In Question 3 of this section I talked about association and disassociation, so I suggest you read this now and then come back to the rest of the answer.)

This process is run by your unconscious and happens automatically. So if, for example, an acquaintance starts talking about being 93, the unconscious bit of your brain will automatically regress to the moment of your cancer diagnosis and trigger the thought that you probably won't make it to 93 – or 63, come to that. If your predisposition is to go into denial, you'll ignore your thoughts and join wholeheartedly in the conversation. If not, you'll experience echoes of the old sadness.

When we don't break out of the familiar cycle, we can suffer from 'chronic grief' – in other words, it never goes away. Sometimes, that can be useful as it reminds us to do what we can to live healthily, but mostly it just makes us feel miserable again. Understanding the process gives us an opportunity to do it differently. You need to set up new thought patterns so that they become your automatic response. When a negative memory is triggered by a conversation, you should say to yourself, 'I've gone there again. Do I need to be there? Is it useful? Has anything different happened since we started talking about retirement?' If the answer (as it will be) is no, you can happily join the conversation with the others. The reality is that they too don't know if they'll make it to their eighties or nineties and nor do you. The difference is that you've had an illness that made you confront your mortality. It has, therefore, become part of your reality, while, for many of your friends, it's not part of theirs. I'm no doctor but I do know that many women survive well into their eighties and nineties in spite of having been diagnosed with cancer when they were younger so take heart.

Now let's consider your friends. I'm sure, as I think you are, that they have no intention of upsetting you. I don't expect it crosses their mind that you still feel sensitive. They may well have held back from this type of conversation when you were unwell but I expect they've decided that now you are better, your life is back to normal. Well, it may very probably be behind you but you know that today's 'normal' is not the same 'normal' of four years ago. They, too, will have gone through the loss and grief reaction curve when you were ill and no doubt at other times in their lives. They may still want to deny this has happened to you or that it could happen to them. They have no intention of being negative: it is just the way they cope.

It sounds as though you're trying to protect them from the uncomfortable feelings raised if you mention your illness and fears. I wonder if that's your normal pattern of behaviour. Do you worry about others more than yourself? (See Section 5, Question 1 on Herrmann thinking preferences.) It's time you put yourself first! I'm not suggesting that you go round scolding them all for being insensitive but I do think it's absolutely valid for you to say how you feel. You may also be helping them to talk about their own mortality. None of us gets to this age without wondering when we'll die and how. And yet, it's still one of the great taboos. You'd be doing them a big favour by encouraging them to air their hopes and fears.

Take a look at the Resource List and Bibliography for places you can get more information. Emotional Freedom Technique (EFT) would be very helpful for you. (See Section 2, Question 3, as well as how to change habits and beliefs in Section 6, Question 4.)

Q5 I have mixed feelings about the prospect of retiring and knowing what to do is becoming a bit of a problem and keeping me awake at night. I know it could give me an opportunity to do something new with my life but I seem to be going round in circles. Do you have any tips on how to approach this gear change in my life?

Over the years, we all learn techniques to solve problems. Our methods become habits and we find ourselves solving every problem in the same tried and tested way. But what's important when trying to solve a problem is lateral thinking. Dr Edward de Bono, a leading authority on problem-solving and creative thinking, divides thinking into two types: vertical and lateral.

Vertical thinking uses logic the traditional way. Lateral thinking involves thinking out of the usual sequence and arriving at a solution from another angle. William J. J. Gordon, another leader in the field, says in *Synectics Theory*, 'The ultimate solutions to problems are rational; the process of finding them is not.'

EXERCISE: LATERAL THINKING

This exercise is a taster in lateral thinking.

1. Find a piece of paper and something to write with.

2. Timing yourself for two minutes, write down as many different things as you can that you can do with a paper bag.

3. Don't limit yourself – anything goes!

4. Now do the same thing for a garden fork.

5. How many ideas did you get?

6. Now apply exactly the same technique to your own problem. Write 'retirement' on a sheet of paper and, with no limitations, write down as many ideas as you can. And yes, anything goes . . .

The problem-solving process has a number of different elements:

Step 1:   Problem definition – in other words, under-standing the problem

Step 2:   Idea generation

Step 3:   Analysis and evaluation of ideas

Step 4:   Decision-making

You're already halfway through. You've done Steps 1 and 2.

Before you move onto Steps 3 and 4, I think it would be helpful to do the questionnaire that follows. It helps identify the skills and difficulties you have when problem-solving. Find somewhere comfortable to sit and then do this questionnaire:

Look at each statement in the list opposite, and decide whether or not you agree that this represents your view. Then circle the appropriate response.

(SA = strongly agree, A = agree, N = neither agree nor disagree, D = disagree, SD = strongly disagree.) Answer all the questions.

1. I can usually understand a problem from other people's viewpoints.	SA A N D SD
2. I try not to come up with stupid suggestions or ideas.	SA A N D SD

3.	Time spent daydreaming can often help in solving a problem.	SA A N D SD
4.	Most people want pretty much the same out of life.	SA A N D SD
5.	Sometimes I have to sleep on a problem before I can make any headway with it.	SA A N D SD
6.	I tolerate wild ducks as long as they all fly in formation.	SA A N D SD
7.	It's worth spending quite a bit of time defining a problem before starting to solve it.	SA A N D SD
8.	I can always spot a winning idea right away.	SA A N D SD
9	I believe that rules are often made to be broken.	SA A N D SD
10.	I can usually sum up people and situations pretty quickly.	SA A N D SD
11.	I don't mind taking a gamble by trying out or working out a way to resolve a situation.	SA A N D SD
12.	Problem-solving is a serious business, really.	SA A N D SD
13.	I often find it useful to visualise the situation in my mind when trying to solve a problem.	SA A N D SD
14.	Some problem-solving techniques just seem to leave you with dozens of half-baked ideas.	SA A N D SD
15.	I am constructive when people criticise my ideas and solutions.	SA A N D SD
16.	I think most people approach problem-solving in much the same way as I do.	SA A N D SD
17.	I often find that the best ideas come out when working under the pressure of imposed deadlines.	SA A N D SD

18. Every problem can be solved by a combination of cash and common sense.	SA A N D SD

Score odd-numbered and even-numbered questions separately. For odd numbers (e.g. 1, 3, 5), an 'SA' response scores 5, down to 1 for 'SD'. For even numbers (e.g. 2, 4, 6), the scoring is reversed: 'SA' scores 1, up to 5 for 'SD'.

The questionnaire addresses three areas where blocks to your creative thinking can exist:

Perceptual blocks
Emotional blocks
Cultural/environmental blocks

Add the scores for the appropriate questions to give your score for each of the three areas, then add the three to give a grand total:

Perceptual questions	1	4	7	10	13	16	score =
Emotional questions	2	5	8	11	14	17	score =
Cultural/environmental questions	3	6	9	12	15	18	score =
							Total score:

The maximum score per area is 30, and the maximum total score is 90. Per area: 6–13 is low; 14–21 medium; 22–30 high.

Perceptual blocks

A low score in this area indicates that your perception – your way of seeing a problem – doesn't enable you to make the best use of your creative ability. It may be that you tend to define problems too rigidly or specifically. People who have strong perceptual blocks to their thinking tend to categorise or label things and are unable to exploit their creativity to the full.

Often this is because our education has emphasised analytical problem-solving methods and fostered the belief that for any problem there is one right answer. Also, our minds are constantly bombarded by stimuli and communications of all kinds. It's natural for our brains to filter out what's unnecessary so that we can focus only on what's important.

We can reduce the perceptual blocks to our creative thinking by considering the following points:

- Time spent defining a problem before attempting to solve it is useful time. Once you've stated the problem clearly, try to re-state it in at least three different ways. This process alone can give rise to totally unexpected avenues of thought.

- Try to understand a problem from all angles. Be aware that there may be a variety of goals and objectives.

- Don't assume that there's only one right way to solve a problem. There are many theories and techniques that help in the creative-thinking process: some may work on a particular problem; some may not. Make sure that you're open to different approaches.

- Develop the use of visualisation in your problem-solving: imagine the problem from every viewpoint and try to 'see' what would be happening if a solution were found.

Emotional blocks

A low score in this area indicates there may be emotional reasons causing internal blocks. Your education or upbringing may have reinforced the belief that not only is there one answer but that there's only one right answer; hence a fear of being thought stupid or foolish for not producing complete or ideal solutions immediately. In fact, sometimes we're guilty of killing our own fragile and newly formed solutions prematurely.

Creative thinking can sometimes be a sloppy process. There's no fixed agenda governing the way ideas are formed. It may be that your sense of good order needs to be relaxed somewhat, or you may need to be aware that 'sleeping on the problem' is not evading the issue but is actually a very productive, considered course of action. Similarly, it may mean that you should, from time to time, relax your mind and allow your heart to determine in what direction your problem-solving should go. Try leaving the evaluation of your ideas until you have a number of them.

Emotional blocks can be reduced by considering the following:

- Allow yourself to have seemingly stupid ideas. They may turn out not to be so stupid when combined with other ideas, or when seen in a different light.

- When stuck on a problem, literally 'sleep on it' or go and have a break. Your subconscious will continue to work on it and you may find that new ideas present themselves when you return to the problem.

- Try to look beyond the first obvious idea that appears to be a winner. Spend time examining alternative solutions.

- Give headspace to new or unusual solutions. Work on the basis that there's a part of every idea that can be used, either by itself or in combination with other ideas.

- Don't worry about the quantity of ideas that techniques such as brainstorming provide. They stimulate the brain to produce yet more ideas and increase the likelihood of finding a new solution.

Cultural/environmental blocks

If you have a low score in this area, it may mean that you've been susceptible to cultural and educational influences on the way you tackle problem-solving, or that there's something in your present environment that isn't conducive to creative thinking.

Unfortunately for some people, school reinforces a belief that humour, fantasy and play have little place in either learning or problem-solving. In addition, a high value is placed on so-called left-brain thinking (reason, logic, analytical thinking) to the detriment of right-brain thinking (feeling, intuition, qualitative judgement). These factors can have a strong influence on our creative-thinking capability.

Our environment may affect us in many ways. It may make us resistant to change, to see or do things differently. We can reduce the impact of the cultural/environmental blocks by looking at the following factors:

- Use fantasy and daydreaming in your creative-thinking process. Imagine what different solutions would look like if they were implemented and envisage how they could be improved.

- Use creative-thinking techniques and solutions. See the Resource List, especially www.edwdebono.com and www.buzancentres.com.

- Have you set up rules or routines that hinder you from getting a fresh viewpoint when you need one? Ask yourself why these rules were set up. Are they still valid, and what is their purpose?

- Bring humour into your problem-solving – it will add a new dimension.

- Try not to be defensive when others criticise your ideas or solutions. Respond positively in a way that stimulates further creative thinking.

- Common sense (and money) are useful tools when you're implementing a solution. However, creative thinking sometimes means throwing away common sense and being open to irrational or previously unacceptable view-points. Sometimes you need to be outrageous.

By understanding how you've solved problems up to now and the blocks that may have held you back, you now have the opportunity to tackle things in a different way.

EXERCISE: LATERAL THINKING (continued)

Continuing the taster in lateral thinking.

7. Analyse and evaluate your list of ideas, eliminating those that aren't feasible.

8. Decide which one you are going to implement first, and by when.

9. When you have completed the first, go back to your list and tackle another.

Other questions in this section and in Sections 5 and 6 will give you further food for thought. If creative thinking and problem-solving interest you, there are some very good books in the Bibliography (especially those by Tony Buzan and Edward de Bono) that will help you develop your thinking.

Q6 **Our youngest child started college this year; the other three are 'boomerang' kids. We've been toying with the idea of moving out of the city and quite possibly out of the UK for a number of years and this seemed the right time to tell our now grown-up family. The kids were horrified. I think they thought we would be here to meet their every need as we always have been. In spite of being a bit put out, I'm now beginning to wonder if we were wrong. When is the right time to move? We can't stay here till we're 90!**

It's so interesting that our kids always think it's us who are the stick-in-the-muds! Your children assumed they're now finally in control of their own lives and, hey presto, you come up with an idea that shakes their foundations and they feel powerless. And, as all of us do when wrong-footed, they respond defensively.

But that doesn't mean that, after some good discussions, they won't feel fine. You don't say when you might be planning to make your move but, as you're still considering the options, I imagine it isn't next week. Young people in my experience find it hard to plan what they're going to do that evening, let alone in a year or two's time! I expect they thought you were off in a couple of months at the latest so I suggest you reassure them that nothing's set in stone.

The concept of a family home is an interesting one. It's obvious that those children who've either been born in the house where they grew up or came to it when they were very little will feel that this place is the family home. However, if you talk to children of parents who've moved about, they see the place where they have a bedroom as the family home. With separated parents, children tend to think of the place where they keep their belongings as home and anywhere else as somewhere they visit.

So what actually makes a family home? In our ideal view, it's the place where nothing bad can happen and all will be cosy. No wonder then that the possibility of this changing can be a bit unsettling. I'm not talking about something rational or tangible but something purely emotional. Your children won't be reacting as adults (see Section 4, Question 1), so they'll need reassuring that, even if your location changes, your and their father's love for them stays the same.

The effect of any move on your children will be proportional to the length of time they've been away from the parental home. Once children are settled in their own homes with their own lives, the likelihood is that your moving from the house will have little effect on them because they'll have created their own familiar environment. They may have something to say if you're planning to move to the other side of the country or even abroad as that may affect how often you see each other but the bricks and mortar will no longer hold the same allure.

Your youngest child has just gone to college and is managing a huge transition in his or her life but will only be there, especially in the first year, for a maximum of 36 weeks, which will be interspersed with weekends at home for someone's birthday or to see old friends. The familiar in their lives is centred on their home, somewhere that needs to remain for them as it's always been.

I worked recently with a client who was in her late forties and yet she still hadn't forgiven her parents for moving without any discussion two months after she'd gone to university. She came 'home' to find no room: she had to sleep in her mother's study and fold the bed up every day! She felt betrayed and claimed this had detrimentally affected her adult life.

Of course you're entitled to your own life, but what's the hurry? Why not give your youngest child a little time to settle into his or her own life before making your move? Otherwise, it might look as if you've been living somewhere where you'd remained just because of them and that's not a nice feeling.

You talk about possibly wanting to move abroad. Ask yourself the following questions (and they might equally apply if you're planning to move elsewhere in the UK).

EXERCISE: MOVING QUIZ

1. Do you want to live out of the UK permanently or would you prefer to split your time? If so, in what proportion?

2. What size property are you looking for – one just for the two of you or one where the family can come and visit?

3. What sort of climate do you want?

4. Are you happy to go somewhere where they speak a different language?

5. Do you want sea, mountains or countryside?

6. How accessible do you want to be?

7. Do you want to be the only Brits there, or do you want to live in an 'expat' community?

8. Do you want to move into a new-build or renovate an old property?

9. Do you want a garden or just a roof terrace? Are you planning to be self-sufficient?

10. Have you taken stock of your finances and worked out what you can afford?

11. Have you looked into medical care and insurance?

12. What are your contingency plans if things don't work out exactly as you expected?

Even we grown-ups can be lured into a false sense of security when we watch the numerous property programmes on TV. I expect you'll find that, by the time you've researched the answers and found a property, your children will be three years older, the youngest in his or her first job, and the others well on the way to being settled but all of them happy to watch you enjoy a new start – and provide a holiday home for them!

Q7 **I'm beginning to find it hard to get out of bed in the morning. My life has become routine. I get up and go to work, where I am bored, the same feeling I experience at home. Nothing much excites me. Retirement is looming. I don't want it to be like this for the rest of my days. Do you have any suggestions on how I can get myself out of this rut?**

What a sorry state of affairs! But there is still hope. Your situation may currently strike you as hopeless but it's not. All the answers already given in this section will help you with your question, starting with self-motivation. Retirement is covered in other parts of this section as well as in Section 5.

Different people are motivated by different things. To re-engage your interest at work and at home, you need to identify what makes you feel good and gives you a buzz, and then concentrate on those things. Abraham Maslow's *Motivation and Personality*, originally written in 1954, remains a definitive work.

He believed it was essential for our mental wellbeing that we fulfil our potential. His 'hierarchy of needs and self-actualisation' is a fundamental concept in psychology.

Maslow said that everyone must have their basic physiological needs met before they can consider anything else. Once this has happened, our need for security becomes paramount. After that comes love, self-esteem and self-actualisation, which he defined as using fully your 'talents, capacities and potentialities'.

In 1961, an American psychologist named David McClelland described three types of motivational needs that come into play after our most basic survival needs are met. These are achievement, affiliation and power. Generally, all three are present in all of us, but in different proportions.

EXERCISE: HOW TO IDENTIFY YOUR PREFERENCES

Under each of the primary motivators there are a total of ten statements. Rate yourself on each of these statements relating to each primary motive. Use a scale of 1–10 with 1 being the least indicative of you and 10 the most indicative:

Achievement motivators

1. I like working by myself and making my own decisions.

2. I like realistic challenges and getting things done.

3. My hobbies are ones where I can measure my performance; I am generally goal-orientated.

4. I'm not one for socially impressive occasions; I have little interest in impressing other people.

5. I don't work well under close supervision.

6. My favourite colours tend to be 'cool' ones like blue and green.

7. In a work situation, it is important I am given the facts and can analyse them and assess the risks.

8. I am punctual and keep to schedules.

9. I like to set challenging goals and targets and meet them by myself.

10. I like business dealings to be to the point; I haven't got much time for chit chat.

Power motivators

1. I am firm and can be direct and competitive; I can be persuasive with others in my dealings.

2. I am active in my organisation's politics. I know 'who's who' and have learnt ways to convince others to accept my ideas.

3. When I join clubs and committees, my preference is to be on the board.

4. I like to have things I have won or acquired on show.

5. I am usually the one chosen to act as a representative and spokesman for other people and to give advice.

6. I drive my car fast.

7. My favourite colours are strong, like red and brown.

8. I enjoy a good argument and like challenging other people at work.

9. I like to take control of the situation and advise others to accept my ideas.

10. I like to form an opinion on any given subject and I'm good at converting other people to my point of view.

Affiliation motivators

1. I actively seek out the company of other people; I like going to places where I can make friends.

2. Being liked as a person is really important to me; I like to interact with friends.

3. I am not very assertive; people would describe me as warm and friendly.

4. I love to talk about my family, friends and interests.

5. My favourite colours are yellow and pale browns.

6. The people I work with are as important as the job. I like a good chat at work and it doesn't need to directly relate to the job in hand.

7. I like to keep conversations going. I'm not keen on silences.

8. I try to create warm, personal relationships with other people wherever I am and whatever their position, even with my boss.

9. I get upset when people are indifferent. If I can, I avoid cool or cold people.

10. I like to know I'm thought well of, accepted and seen as sincere.

How to score

Add up your score for each group. The highest you can have is 100, the lowest 10.

The highest figure gives you an idea of which motive is a driving force behind your behaviour.

For example, if your score is Achievement 90, Power 78 and Affiliation 36, you will be motivated by reaching your goals and being noticed for it.

If, however, your score is Achievement 62, Power 27 and Affiliation 86, you will be motivated by being with a good group of people and you won't want to be noticed for what you do.

Clearly, we all want to have our needs met. These act as internal drivers which spark us into action. If we don't get our needs met, we end up disenchanted, bored and possibly depressed. The converse is true, too: if we get an extra buzz from an activity we will be all the more willing to do it. So, having done the questionnaire, you now know what motivates you.

The next step is to choose your five highest-scoring statements and your five lowest-scoring statements. Let's imagine a high one is, 'Being liked as a person is really important to me. I like to interact with friends.' Ask yourself the following questions:

- What am I doing to meet this need?

- What would be three good things to do to ensure this need is met?

- What are the first steps I need to take for each of the three and by when could I hope to achieve my goals?

- Create a specific plan for each.

- Make sure you've thought of how you will celebrate achieving any or all of these targets.

OK, now pick a lowest-scoring statement, for example, 'I enjoy a good argument and like challenging other people at work.' Ask yourself:

- How often do I have to do this at work?

- Who can I talk to about it to change this attitude?

- What other things can I do to help things shift?

- What am I going to do if things don't change, as it is quite clearly draining me?

- How will I celebrate when I have achieved it?

I know that, when we're fed up, it's hard to galvanise ourselves into action but I'd recommend that you do the above exercise alongside the others in this section and I'm pretty sure you'll find yourself out there doing things that make you want to dance and sing. If, for any reason, you really can't shift this feeling, go and talk to your GP and/or a life coach or counsellor.

Good luck!

❧ Section Two ❧

You're Never Too Old to ... Look Good

I n recent years, more and more concerns expressed by clients and readers alike have been to do with how they look. It's not hard to work out why. Books, magazines and TV programmes seem to be increasingly obsessed with how we present ourselves to the world, something that is felt as keenly by the insecure teenager as by the woman staring 50 or 60 in the face.

By 2007, according to an internet report by market-research group Mintel, Britons were spending more money on cosmetic surgery than they were on tea. That figure was predicted to exceed £659 million in 2007 and £912 million by 2009. Non-surgical procedures are the most popular options. Their research suggests that as many as 100,000 Botox® injections are carried out in the UK every year. But other procedures are catching up fast. Figures from the British Association of Aesthetic Plastic Surgeons (available on the internet) show that anti-ageing surgical procedures increased from just over 6,000 in 2005 to just over 9,000 the following year.

And it's not only surgery. A recent Boots internet report revealed that UK women spend over £650 million on anti-ageing products each year. Nor does all of this apply exclusively to women. Apparently, almost 10 per cent of anti-ageing products are purchased by men and a similar percentage of plastic surgery procedures are carried out on men. Sales of cosmetics and skincare aimed at men grew by more than 40 per cent between 1998 and 2003.

We could argue into the night about whether you should celebrate the lines on your face as evidence of life's rich tapestry or whether you should take advantage of the advances in medical technology. But the inescapable fact remains that, rightly or wrongly, more people than ever worry about their outward appearance, as these typical questions demonstrate.

Q1 Every morning, when I get up, I dread looking in the mirror and seeing my face. If I manage to avoid the mirror, I don't feel I'm any older than when I was in my twenties. But, as soon as I look, I see a 58-year-old going on 90! When everyone else is away, I cover the mirror so I won't see myself first thing in the morning. I know this is a bit odd. What can I do about it?

It's easy as we get older to hanker after a time in our lives when we imagined we looked effortlessly lovely. As you know by looking at old photographs, this is almost certainly not the case. So, forget about the past and concentrate on the world as it is, not as it was. Accentuating the positive is the only course of action, not just to make you happier, but healthier too.

For a start, it can be surprisingly cheering to remember all the 'firsts' you'll never have to go through again. Just imagine having to sit for all those exams, taking your driving test, having your first period. Thank goodness all that's behind you! Of course, there are undeniably moments we all wish we could experience again like meeting our first love, giving birth to our first child, visiting Paris or Sydney or Rome for the first time. If you go to Section 1, Question 3 there are some tips on how you can enjoy those feelings all over again. Now, let's focus on your face for a moment. I am reminded of a favourite story by Rose Mula, called 'The Stranger in My House':

> A very weird thing has happened – a strange old lady has moved into my house.
>
> I have no idea who she is, where she came from or how she got in. I certainly didn't invite her. All I know is that one day she wasn't there and the next day she was.
>
> She is a clever old lady and manages to keep out of sight for the most part but, whenever I pass a mirror, I catch a glimpse of her and, whenever I look in the mirror to check my appearance, there she is hogging the whole thing, completely obliterating my gorgeous face and body.
>
> This is very rude!

(abridged from Mula, Rose, 2003)

If it's true that beauty is in the eye of the beholder, the first beholder who needs to see you as beautiful is yourself. Once you can do that, then you're no longer dependent on others to make you feel good. And you CAN do it for yourself. You CAN be as beautiful as you feel.

The magic of this is that, as soon as you see yourself as beautiful, so do others. It's infectious and has nothing to do with how you look in relation to any perceived stereotype. We also often foolishly compare ourselves with others but, as each person is unique, comparisons are as futile as they are irrelevant.

All our lives we will have known someone who is taller, younger, prettier, fatter, thinner or with glossier hair than our own. This can drive us mad and get us nowhere. We've also probably known people we considered to be much less attractive than ourselves and yet who landed someone everyone else wanted. So why not try the following exercise in photo-gazing.

EXERCISE: PICTURE THIS

1. Gather together some photographs of yourself at different ages. Ideally, every five years.

2. Take a look at how you looked at different stages of your life. What did your face look like? Did all the haircuts suit you? Did you have spots at some point? What about your hair colour and your make-up? As dispassionately as possible, ask yourself which styles and colours suit you best.

3. Make a list of three good points and three not-so-special ones for each decade up to the present day. Focus on even the smallest features such as your teeth or your long eyelashes.

4. Take note that even in your youth you had bits you didn't like. Now discard that list – you don't need it any more.

5. Focus on your list of your great points, which can be used whenever you feel low in confidence or are having a bad hair day. And don't feel ashamed about keeping the list in your purse or handbag so that you can refer to it at will and remind yourself that you're doing all right.

Self-evidently, it's true that our looks change as we get older. But, as we've seen (in Section 1, Question 2), if our expectations don't meet reality there is inevitably a feeling of disappointment. Therefore, it makes sense to set yourself a different goal for this next stage of life. Some things may stay the same but it's better to accept that, of course, some things will change. Take a look through some photographs in magazines and newspapers and begin to create a realistic vision of the face you would like to have. Take that picture with you when you next go for a haircut or makeover.

I met a friend the other day who is over 70. She looked fantastic. When I told her this, she said the only difference between looking great at 70 and great at 30 was that getting ready to go out now takes longer. If making up is your thing (and it isn't everyone's), you may have to spend more time than you did when you were younger and probably more money on the creams and cosmetics involved. You may also benefit from additional advice on products and colours that will suit your changing skin tone.

Many department stores offer free makeovers. Plan a day out, ideally with a friend, and both have your faces done. Learn what you can do that will make you look and feel good. A lot of the women I talk to tell me they're still doing their make-up as they always did. Perhaps now might be the moment to get someone else to take you in hand. Who knows? You might even be able to face the bathroom mirror in the morning!

Q2 Last week, I went shopping and bought what I thought was a really trendy but suitable dress. I have a good figure and have always been able to wear whatever I want. Back home, I put on the dress prior to going out for the evening and came downstairs. My daughter took one look and said, 'Oh, please!' When I asked her what the problem was, she said, 'You're fifty-six, Mum, not twenty-six!' I went back upstairs feeling terrible. Was she right? Should I now be dressing like my own mother? I don't want to look old.

Our children certainly know how to make us feel bad, don't they?

When we think of grown-ups, whatever our own age is, we tend to conjure up people who are stereotypically grey-haired, who wear tweed skirts to the knee, teamed with sensible shoes, thick stockings and plain twinsets. They're neat and tidy. They talk in dulcet tones and do all the right things. They save money, eat sensibly, go for walks, never stay up too late, drink too much and so on. For many of us, this is never how we've behaved and it's unlikely we're going to start now.

There's nothing that says we have to change our behaviour because we've hit a certain age. Those of us who are modest, sensible and unassuming were probably like that when we were three and those of us who weren't never will be. As Doris Lessing said in the *Sunday Times* Books section in 1992, 'The great secret that all old people share is that you really haven't changed in seventy or eighty years. Your body changes but you don't change at all. And that, of course, causes great confusion.'

Having said all that, mutton dressed as lamb is not special! But even in the south of France (which always seems to me to give licence to the older woman to dress as she wishes), there are those who do it with style and those who don't. The question here is whether your daughter was right or whether she has an image of what mothers *should* look like. Either way, she didn't see what she expected to. On the other hand, perhaps she hit a raw nerve precisely because you weren't sure yourself. Did her comment maybe echo that inner critical voice (see Section 4, Question 1, the inner parent) which says women of a certain age should look a certain way?

My advice would be that, if you know she's right, return the dress and get your money back. Before you do that, though, follow the exercise later in this question so you know you're taking it back because you believe it isn't for you and doesn't fit with how *you* want to be and not because of what your daughter said.

When going shopping, it's a good idea to take a friend with you whose dress sense you like so you have a woman of your own age on hand to give unbiased advice. We've all had shopping disasters where we've allowed ourselves to believe an over-eager assistant and come home with something that, even before we've laid it out on the bed, we know in our hearts isn't right.

I did once go to a large department store and asked to see a stylist as I was aware that I needed to take stock of my wardrobe. The assistant instantly called me 'madam' and adopted a look and voice which said to me, 'Well, at your age . . .' This might, of course, have been my paranoia but I'm sure she would have presented a very different attitude to a 19-year-old. Maybe that is one of the reasons that many of us find ourselves drawn to shops that are no longer (or may never have been) quite suitable for us. The assistants here neither mirror our age nor care how old we are. They're just happy if we buy something. I think what's clear is that, if we feel confident and believe in ourselves and know we look good, no one will rattle us and put us off our stride. (See Section 3, Question 1.)

There are lots of books about ageing and how to dress, and shops and department stores that will offer advice on how to look good, so search the internet for what's relevant to you. What I do know is that many of us get into a habit and assume that what has suited us before and made us feel we looked good will go on doing so. But we change – in weight, in skin tone and so on – and we should adapt our style to match these changes, while still keeping in fashion.

The clothes we wear, the hairstyles and colours we choose are all statements of which version of us we want to present to the world on any given occasion. I remember years ago, when I worked in a number of different environments, that I would regularly arrive on the station platform and bump into a friend's husband, and he, rather than greeting me in the conventional way, would announce when he looked at me whom it was I'd be working with that day. And he was almost always spot on!

I would never have turned up at the marble reception hall of an investment bank in the jeans I might have worn if working with a community group. Neither is better or worse than the other but we dress for a purpose and I wanted to fit in with the culture of the organisation I was visiting. Our clothes, our chosen style, change to meet the setting. Some of us will stick closely to a style – classic, smart, casual, arty, glamorous and so on – while others will dip into a few of these.

The following is a step-by-step guide to help you decide how you want to dress:

EXERCISE: WHO, WHAT, WEAR?

1. Ask yourself the question: what image do I want to portray?

   - At work

   - Out with friends

   - At home

   - Special occasion

2. Write down what kind of clothes you would wear for each situation.

3. Now imagine yourself in each of those situations dressed like that.

4. Think about your assets. Which bits are you pleased with? Do you have good breasts but a round tummy? Well, flaunt the breasts in a good, uplifting bra and no one will notice the tummy! If you have good legs, don't always wear trousers and long skirts. We all have some bits of our body that are better than others, so make the most of them. Make the picture bright and bold and colourful: as if you were in a Hollywood movie. You're the star!

5. It's important to give yourself some movement. Step into her and become her; walk and move around like her. Change anything you aren't happy with so that you become the ideally dressed you. Are you giving the impression you want to give? Do this for each of the different situations. Is there a theme?

6. Now take a look in your wardrobe and do that overdue clear-out! Do this for clothes, belts, shoes, scarves, everything.

   Divide them into:

   • Fit the bill perfectly

   • Some hope with altering

   • Could be used for the chores

   • No-hopers

7. Now, having done it once, go through the perfect pile. Pick up each item and name two occasions when you can honestly see yourself wearing these clothes and accessories. If you can't, chuck whatever it is into the 'no-hopers' bag. Do the same for the altering pile and the ones you might wear if there was nothing else in the wardrobe and no one was coming round.

I know this is hard because last week I finally came to the realisation that a belt I wore and loved in my thirties just doesn't fit. My weight is no different but my shape is. Having very reluctantly decided to discard it, I had a thought – 'What is it I really love about it?' and the answer was the buckle! So now I'm having it stitched on to a new, bigger belt. The cost will be a quarter of buying a new one. Bearing that in mind, take one last look at the discard pile and make sure you haven't missed something that could be altered.

If you haven't done this for a while, you're probably now horrified at the pile to discard. But remember that, if you hang on to everything, you'll be perpetuating the person you don't want to be. I understand that you may now have a limited wardrobe, but you'll have one that says who you are.

And don't worry about acquiring new items of clothing. It needn't cost a fortune. In every town, there are now numerous charity shops where others like you will have taken their perfectly good clothes that no longer create the appropriate image for them. Take a look when you drop your bag in and see what you can find. There are also lots of 'nearly new' shops and second-hand designer shops where, for a quarter of the price, you can pick up some fantastic bargains.

We're talking quality rather than quantity. I've never heard anyone say, when looking at someone beautifully dressed, that she shouldn't wear that outfit so often. Use accessories cleverly. A different belt and scarf can make an outfit look completely different.

Now back to your daughter. Once you've really worked out for yourself what it is that makes you feel good, you're unlikely to be so thrown by an unkind remark. Have a chat with her and ask her what it was that made her so aghast. Explain to her that it hurt and that, even though you aren't young in her eyes, you feel – just in the same way she does – that feelings don't age. Do a mental check for yourself that you've never said something similar to her. Look with her at how you can give each other advice in a way that it can be heard, assessed and acted on, if appropriate. (See Section 4, Question 1 and Section 3, Question 4, communication and assertiveness.)

Q3 **My partner took me out last week to buy a ring for my birthday. I was thrilled until we got to the shops. I haven't really focused on my hands before. As I started trying on rings, I was confronted by what looked like my**

mother's hands. I felt so old and sad and not like buying anything. I just stood there in the shop with tears running down my cheeks. My partner had no idea what was going on. We ended up having a row. I feel bad about it but I hate all this ageing stuff. How can I feel better about myself so I can accept how I am and that I will get older? In my head, I'm still 18. In my body, I'm 59. How do I reconcile this?

Hands are quite clearly an issue for many. I expect you saw the newspaper report in which Madonna was purported to have had her hands 'replaced' in publicity pictures or airbrushed so the wrinkles didn't show. Hands, like necks, are two parts of the body which betray a person's age. As we get older, the plumpness that we see in a toddler's hands disappears as our hands become bonier and veined. They inevitably become less elastic and suffer from sunspots so it's no surprise that yours are showing your age.

I wonder if you've heard of a technique called Emotional Freedom Technique (EFT) which I think could be really helpful in dealing with your feelings about growing older. EFT is based on balancing the natural flow of the body's energy system. If you've ever had a bad hair day where your hair appears to be 'electric', you'll know that your body contains a great deal of energy. When the energy flows smoothly, we feel good; when it gets blocked, we feel below par. EFT has its roots in ancient Chinese medicine. It works through stimulating the energy meridians (as used in acupuncture), a network of pathways that traverse the body and through which invisible energy flows.

EFT is a non-needle version of acupuncture. By tapping on the ends of meridian points, it's possible to move energy along and help it flow through the body. The fundamental belief behind EFT, which was founded by Gary Craig, is that 'The cause of all negative emotions is a disruption in the body's energy system,' and that, while these remain unresolved, they cause physical and emotional pain and illness.

Craig's lifelong interest in personal improvement psychology led him to the field of energy therapy. In the 1920s, Albert Einstein stated that everything (including our bodies) is composed of energy. Craig studied with Roger Callahan, a clinical psychologist who discovered that stimulating the acupressure points by touch enabled his patients to deal with and dispel long-held phobias. Callahan explored through his therapeutic work the energy factors behind the common conflict that we have between wanting to change something and our resistance to that change. Gary Craig has built on this and produced a clear and simple formula that has remarkable success rates. He's written extensively on a diverse range of emotional and physical issues and has produced a wealth of material. To find out more go to the Resource List and download the free manual at www.emofree.com, and see also Section 5, Question 3.

We all have misgivings about growing older. That can cause breaks in our energy system – much like a break in the Christmas tree lights' electrical circuit – and a negative emotion is set up. If it's a severe break in our body's energy flow, we can end up physically sick or emotionally out of sorts. If it's less severe, it goes on working like the lights: they're all right if you don't touch them, but they can remain unpredictable unless the root problem is addressed.

EFT has a very clear, easy-to-learn routine which combines articulating the problem with tapping. It's important to note that no EFT practitioner would say that it replaces medical treatment for physical or mental health problems. But many EFT practitioners have had remarkable results in even long-standing physical and emotional disease. If doing it on yourself, you should be as careful as you would be if you were practising a yoga handstand at home or swimming in a pool without a lifeguard – stay in the shallow end!

Let's now go through the basic steps so you can tap on your negative feelings. For example, lack of confidence in your body (see Section 3, Question 3) is a problem that might be solved by employing this technique.

EXERCISE: CREATING POSITIVE FEELINGS

1. Start by thinking of the problem and rating the intensity of your feelings on a scale from 0 to 10 (0 being least and 10 being most). Based on your reaction in the jeweller's, I'd go for a 10!

2. Take a look at the diagrams and get ready to tap. You can use either hand and you tap by using your index and middle fingers.

3. Start by tapping the karate chop point continuously (see diagram) and say the 'set-up statement'. In your case, it would be something like 'Even though I feel sad and at a loss when I think about ageing, I completely accept myself.' (You can, of course, adapt this to use for any problem or a difficult memory.)

    The 'set-up statement' has two parts to it: it clearly states the problem and then adds a positive affirmation. This helps to put your body into a receptive state and stops you adding all the negative bits (for example, 'I will now feel good about my age,' before adding, 'No, I won't because of x, y and z'). This two-part process is known as psychological reversal and it stops your unconscious working against your conscious mind.

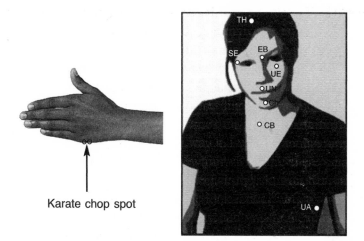

Karate chop spot

4. You then tap each point (see diagram) up to seven times while repeating the negative bit of the statement – in this case, 'Feel sad and at a loss when I think about ageing.'

The sequence is: end of eyebrow near nose (EB); side of eye on bone, i.e. other end of eyebrow (SE); under eye (UE); under nose (UN); chin, in the dip under mouth (Ch); collarbone (CB); under arm (UA); and top of the head (TH).

> Eyebrow: I'm sad about my age
> Side of eye: I'm sorry I'm ageing
> Under eye: I don't like ageing
> Under nose: I feel old
> Chin: I feel sad I'm ageing
> Collarbone: I don't like my age
> Under arm: I don't like my ageing hands
> Top of head: I'm sorry about my age

5. Then tap stating what you would prefer, rather than what you are continually experiencing. This allows you to put the positive into the system. So in this case:

Eyebrow: I feel good about my hands
Side of eye: I like looking at my hands
Under eye: I appreciate how well my hands work
Under nose: I have let go of the fear of ageing
Chin: I adore receiving and giving gifts
Collarbone: I welcome this new ring
Under arm: I like being this age
Top of head: I enjoy my life and relationships

6. Now take a deep breath and go back and think of the moment in the shop. Ask yourself if you'd still score 10 points – or something lower.

7. Unless you went to zero, continue tapping for several rounds but this time start the round with 'My remaining feelings about not wanting to age.' So you acknowledge that the negative feeling remains but it's now different from how it was. And see what happens.

I'm sure for many of you the idea of tapping on acupressure points sounds odd and unlikely to be of any use. All I can say is, give it a go! If you find it helps, do it again; if not, move on to something else. There's some information on how to learn more on EFT at the back of the book and a wealth of information on the internet (www.emofree.com). Sometimes, if the problem is resistant, it's a good idea to find an experienced practitioner to work with you on your negative issues. One of the things I've found for myself as well as my clients is that a combination of both works well. Getting help from someone else and then continuing the tapping on a daily basis between sessions really does help get results.

Q4 **I'm 55 years old. I had an uncomfortable experience last week and it isn't the first time it's happened. I was walking down the street, chatting with my**

two daughters, and I noticed people (mainly men) looking at them in an admiring way but not even registering me. I'm increasingly aware that I'm becoming invisible and I don't like it!

You're not the first and you certainly won't be the last person over 50 to say this. And yet, I'm curious. What exactly do you want to be visible for and to whom? Are you really saying that you want to be eyed up in the street by strangers? Because you could easily do that by wearing something outrageous or completely unsuitable. I can guarantee you'd be noticed!

I think you've got a bit confused. I'm sure you're noticed by everyone who matters to you. Your girls, for example, certainly notice you for who you are and want to walk down the street with you. They're not ashamed of you and how you look. Ask any young woman if she wants her mother to look the same as her and see how she reacts. What she wants is for her mother to look like a mum. That doesn't mean dowdy; it just means dressed appropriately for her age.

I remember when I was about seventeen, going out with my family and friends. The other mother was in her mid-sixties. She was dressed in a lovely outfit in muted colours, worn with a flowing scarf. Her make-up was expertly applied and her hair well cut. It was grey and she'd made no attempt to colour it. As we walked into the restaurant every head turned, young and old, to look at her. Her poise and self-belief were magnetically appealing: no one noticed her age. That was a seminal moment for me.

I agree it's sometimes hard not looking 24 any more and especially when that's how old we feel in our heads. What many of us find it hard to do is reconcile our vision and reality.

(See Section 1, Question 2 about unrealistic expectations.) I'm sure you're extremely proud of your girls and are thrilled that others, like you, admire them, but it sounds as though you might be a bit envious of your daughters. It can be hard accepting that your youth is behind you. Some women even feel in competition with their children, something with the serious potential to sour the relationship. What do people think of me? If you're unsure of the answer, try this little exercise.

EXERCISE: FEEDBACK

I. Choose four to six people who you think will be honest about you.

2. Send them an email/letter asking if they'd be happy to do this test with you. You can offer to do it for them, too.

3. Ask them if they'd rather answer in person or in writing. Suggest that either way you'd like to talk to them about their answers afterwards.

4. Send them these questions:

   - If I was meeting one of your friends at a restaurant, and they didn't know me, how would you describe me?

   - What do you think are my most striking features?

   - Which of my outfits do you think I look best in and why?

   - If I wanted to make myself more visible, what would you recommend?

- If I were at a party with new people, what do you think they'd notice about me?

- What do you value most about me in our friendship?

- What do you think is unique about me?

- If you were to give me one piece of advice about what to wear or how to do my make-up/hair, what would it be?

- If you were to give me one piece of advice on my behaviour and attitudes, what would it be?

5. When they've replied, read the answers and make a list of your ten most special points. What could you do, if anything, to enhance these?

6. Now look at any not-so-special points. What can you do to improve these?

To ensure we improve our performance, both in our daily working life and in our personal lives, we need time to prepare and plan. This involves asking ourselves the right questions in the right sequence. Where do I want to focus and why?

We will only do something differently or better if we're committed to making the change, recognising and believing in the personal benefits which will more than compensate for the discipline and effort required. Develop a series of goals that will help you to project yourself positively and increase your visibility. When choosing your goals, follow the acronym SMART: Specific, Measurable, Achievable and Agreed, Relevant, Time-bound. A newer version is SMARTER, more powerful and relevant for the modern world because it includes an essential philosophical aspect: Specific, Measurable, Achievable and Agreed, Realistic, Time-bound, Ethical and Exciting, Reviewed.

Objectives are clear, precise forecasts of what you want to achieve in the future. An objective has certain known qualities.

- It has two parts to it: a forecast of the aims to be achieved; and indicators of success.

- It must be realistic and possible to achieve in the time span.

- It should be challenging and pitched at a realistic level of achievement (and produce authentic feelings of satisfaction if you succeed).

- Indicators of success are ways of measuring that the objective has been achieved.

The final step is to develop an action plan. This means determining the sequence of actions to be taken and the deadlines that need to be met to achieve the objective(s).

Additional questions to ask oneself at this stage are:

- Who can provide me with support and help?

- How would I like that support to be given?

- Who will be my 'external conscience' to whom I give explicit 'nagging rights'?

- How will I celebrate?

Once you start doing this and really focus on what you've got and not on what you haven't, you'll find people may well be staring at this 'together' woman in her mid-fifties whom it's impossible to ignore!

Q5 **My two closest friends have just started having Botox® injections. When we went out recently, everyone remarked how well and youthful they looked. No one noticed me – not the norm. It began to make me wonder if 'well' means 'young'? If so, should I be following their example? Or can we stay looking attractive without artificial interventions?**

Sounds to me as though you're feeling a bit sorry for yourself. So the first thing is to stop it! I know that's easier said than done but, if you're finding this tricky, then take a look at Section 1, Question 3.

You also seem to be saying that it's unusual for your friends to be looked at rather than you. Does this mean that you're often seen by people as the most attractive in any group so this was something out of the norm? If that's the case, take a minute to think about how they must feel whenever you and they go out. The following exercise is helpful if you want to 'know' what's going on in someone's head.

EXERCISE: OTHER PEOPLE'S SHOES

1. Find a quiet place to stand, with a bit of space around you. Imagine you're standing in front of your friends before their treatment. See them standing there as you watch them. Behave as you normally would when you're with them. Really feel it.

2. Now stand in one of your friends' spaces and pretend to be her. Take a look at yourself and your other friend.

Stand as she does; be as she is. What does she think
when she sees you? And when she looks at the other
friend? Look at yourself and your friend through her eyes
and mind.

3. Now come out of that space and move into the other
   friend's place. Repeat the same exercise.

4. Come back to your place and be yourself again. What do
   you see now when you see your friends? How do they
   feel when they see you? Check with yourself whether you
   ever do anything that makes them feel lacking in confidence. If so, make a pact with yourself that you won't do
   it again.

5. Now repeat the whole exercise. This time, however,
   imagine them post-Botox® when you move into their
   places. What did you discover this time? Did you find
   you behaved differently because you assumed they would
   look better? Did they behave more confidently because
   they felt better about themselves?

6. Now focus on what you can do to make yourself feel
   good (because that's what matters here). How we think
   about ourselves has a huge effect on how we're seen.

Whatever situation you're in, getting into others' shoes and seeing
the world through their eyes is important. (See Section 3, Question
4.) This exercise can be used whenever you find yourself wanting
to know what's going on for someone else. As soon as you're
in their shoes and start to feel what they're feeling, you'll know
what to do to rectify things.

I sometimes employ this device when I'm in a meeting or in a
one-to-one conversation when the discussion is not going very

well. I excuse myself for a moment and pop to the loo. I then do the exercise – getting into the other person's head and trying to understand better what they're thinking and feeling. On my return, I invariably feel in a better position to achieve a positive outcome to whatever is the problem.

Communication is a two-way process and we can wait for the other person to make it better or we can take responsibility and try to achieve it ourselves. In a situation like the one you describe, it's easy to tell yourself you feel bad and then to play out that scenario – a self-fulfilling prophecy.

Now, having dealt with the emotional side of your problem, let's focus on the practical: anti-ageing products, nips and tucks and so on. The anti-ageing industry is big business. Currently, the global anti-ageing market is estimated to be worth approximately $50 billion a year, a figure that is rising all the time.

There's been a big rise in the number of people opting for cosmetic surgery. The British Association of Aesthetic Plastic Surgeons, a non-profit-making organisation established for the advancement of education and practice of plastic surgery for public benefit, reported that a total of 28,921 procedures were carried out in 2006 by BAAPS members in their private practices. (Cosmetic surgery is rarely offered on the NHS.) This represented a 31.2 per cent rise over the previous year. I discuss cosmetic surgery in some depth in Question 6 of this section.

Women had 92 per cent of all cosmetic procedures in the UK in 2006. Anti-ageing procedures proved the most popular, something the figures for 2006 clearly demonstrate: blepharoplasty (eyelid surgery) 5,065 – up 48 per cent on the previous year; face/neck lift 3,281 – up 44 per cent; brow lifts 868 – up 50 per cent.

As well as the more interventionist approaches, there are a myriad other things you can do. Skin-peeling can lighten discoloured areas and freckles, electrodessication can deal with broken veins on the face or leg, dermabrasion can reduce marks and fine lines around the mouth, laser wrinkle treatment can stimulate the production of collagens and fill out lines, sclerotherapy can eliminate thread veins, Botox® helps smooth out foreheads and reduce wrinkles, Restylane® can fill fine lines, non-surgical face lifts using mini-electrodes stimulate the muscles while there are numerous other line- and lip-fillers and plumpers. Additionally, there are, of course, all the products and procedures such as face masks, pressure spray-toning, ozone therapy and every sort of anti-ageing cream you can imagine.

Currently, anti-ageing products account for the biggest share of the skincare market, valued by Euromonitor at €38.3 billion worldwide (www.marketresearch.com). Naturally, the fact that these creams, masks and scrubs are in such demand is proof of how important the anti-ageing segment is to the cosmetic industry.

You ask whether you can be attractive as well as look your age. Yes, you can. But this isn't the message the cosmetic firms put out. These huge multinational companies have not been slow to exploit our superficial insecurities with more and more new products advertised daily.

There is pressure on us all to look younger especially when we see the more mature celebrity looking wrinkle-free in newspapers and magazines. Most of us forget about airbrushing when confronted with these images. In an article in the *Scotsman* in October 2006, Emma More, a beauty therapy lecturer at Telford College in Edinburgh, pointed out that no cream exists which will ever rub away wrinkles entirely. Until relatively recently, there were no products targeted for people in their sixties and seventies. However, things are changing as the baby boomers reach that age.

The growth of the anti-ageing market has led to the global launch of *Elixir*, a glossy magazine that its publisher says is devoted to 'helping you live longer, healthier and happier' lives. The editorial focus for the publication is anti-ageing and rejuvenation products and services, covering all product launches from the world's leading cosmetic companies. The magazine is now available in the UK and aimed predominantly at educated, high-income households.

And then there's hair – do you or don't you colour? I was talking to a woman the other day who said she had gone white by the time she was 33. She loved it then but, once in her late forties, she realised it was ageing her so, after over a decade of being white, she became a brunette. Some might say this was the slippery slope to never seeing yourself as looking all right when older. But who's to say if that's a good or a bad thing? In the end, it must be a personal choice.

What I do know is that, if you want to go down the route of cosmetic surgery, do your research as thoroughly as possible and only go to a qualified professional practitioner. Yes, they may be more expensive and that's why!

If you're thinking of buying products, do so sparingly. If they don't seem to make any difference, don't buy them again. Also, try to ensure that whatever you do makes *you* feel good and that you aren't doing it to compete with others or to please someone else. If you feel good inside, this radiates outwards and no one will notice the odd wrinkle or two.

We started this question talking about Botox®. Interestingly, I heard a Hollywood casting director talking before the 2007 Oscars about three of the nominated films that starred women in their fifties, sixties and seventies. She said there was a trend for films about older people but it was now difficult to find enough actors of 50+ whose faces still moved naturally. No point having an actor who looks ten years younger than his or her age but who couldn't show any emotion!

Q6 **I'm finding myself less and less happy with my body. I watch every nip-and-tuck TV programme about plastic surgery. But I'm a bit worried – if I went down that road, would it be successful and would I ever be able to stop? How do I decide what to do?**

I am going to focus my answer on plastic surgery, the pluses and the minuses. Your question also touches on how to look and feel good on both the inside and outside. (See Section 2, Question 1.)

Television programmes such as *Extreme Makeover* and *10 Years Younger* can certainly make it all seem very appealing and possible but, inevitably, they over-simplify the procedure. Plastic surgery itself has existed for many years and has been used to correct disfigurements from deformities, accidents, including those of war, and disease. Many incredibly successful techniques were developed to enable people with severe disfigurements and disabilities to cope better with their lives.

But what you're asking about is cosmetic surgery. It's certainly true that baby boomers are turning increasingly to cosmetic surgery, which is why it's such a highly successful industry. It's also true that in the West the over-fifties have more disposable income than any other age group in society and more than previous generations. With the possibility of more healthy years in which to work and play, it's little wonder that people are taking extra trouble over their appearance. Interestingly, it is not just those in their fifties and sixties who are seeking to look better; there are also 80-year-olds opting for surgery.

Surgery for purely cosmetic reasons is not offered on the NHS and is expensive. It is also, like any surgery, not without risks and we have all heard of disasters. Therefore, it's not something to undertake lightly. The first thing to ask yourself is why you want it done. What is it about your appearance that you don't like? Is it something that is preoccupying you all of the time? Or is it something that you only think about when you watch TV programmes or on a bad day? Is it a real desire or a whim? I'm sure there's hardly a 50+ woman who hasn't pulled back the skin on her face and thought, 'Mmm . . . that would look good!' Most, however, let go and get on with their day. Do you think that, if you opt for some sort of face lift, for instance, your life will change and you'll feel better about yourself? Often it is not as simple as that. There will be other things going on in your life.

Are you feeling unattractive and finding it difficult to find a new relationship? Or do you worry perhaps that you're not seen as sexy in an existing relationship? You need to ask yourself whether it's because you look a bit older or are there other things going on that could be the cause – for example, generally feeling fed up with life because you're in a rut or the fact that you're not going out enough to meet new people.

Cosmetic surgery by itself won't make you feel more loved or more popular. Talking to a life coach or counsellor about this may help you change your internal feelings and, consequently, your external appearance. We all know that, when we're feeling down, we don't usually present our best face. On the other hand, if you're contemplating going under the knife because someone else has said that you should and then they'll fancy you, you need to think very carefully. I don't think it's as simple as that. Talk to whoever it is about their feelings as well as getting some relationship counselling.

If you're considering cosmetic surgery because you think you look too old to get a new job or you're being sidelined because you look the oldest in the office, remember that it's now illegal in the UK for employers to discriminate on grounds of age. (Please read Section 5, Question 4.) If you want to change careers, talk to a careers counsellor or, if you feel bullied at work, talk to your manager or the HR department. See www.workingcareers.com and the General Resource List for career advice.

Also, consider less drastic, non-surgical cosmetic treatments such as Botox® or dermal fillers such as Restylane® that might do the trick instead. (I've mentioned these in Question 5 of this section.)

However, if you're genuinely distressed by what you see in the mirror and you don't think you'll learn to appreciate your lines for what they are – lines that show a wealth of experience and knowledge of life and living – then cosmetic surgery may well be for you. Do approach it with caution. Seek out good information from qualified professionals. Cosmetic surgery is now so popular the Department of Health even has a website dedicated to it: www.dh.gov.uk/en/policyandguidance/healthandsocialcaretopics/cosmeticsurgery.

A good place to start is with your GP, who knows your medical history and will also know good local resources. Make sure the clinic is registered with the Healthcare Commission and that you're talking to someone who's medically qualified. Check out the surgeon's qualifications and experience and ask as many questions as you want: you're paying for the service. Very often, we find ourselves tongue-tied when talking to doctors and don't ask as many questions as we would if we were buying, say, a washing machine. If that's true of you, write your questions down and remember to refer to them.

Check out what scarring there may be. There's bound to be some if you have surgery. Also, discuss the risks associated with an anaesthetic, aftercare and risk of infection. The British Association of Aesthetic Plastic Surgeons (BAAPS) has a list of registered surgeons who have to meet strict criteria so they're a useful place to start. If you decide to have the surgery abroad, because it can be cheaper, remember that you need to be sure that the practitioner is fully qualified and experienced. The BAAPS is also a good place to start when looking for non-UK practitioners as they list recommended clinics overseas.

You were concerned that, if you embarked on cosmetic surgery, you might not know when to stop. I must admit, this made my alarm bells ring. If you know that you've got bags under your eyes, for example, and you hate them and having them removed will make you feel better, then you wouldn't have doubts about getting 'addicted' to surgery.

But, if you're saying that you don't like how you look because you simply haven't come to terms with the fact that you're getting older, I'd advise caution. There's no such thing as the perfect body. Why we think we can have one when we're 70, when we didn't have one when we were 20, I'll never understand. We have all seen movie stars who can't move their faces: they may look younger but they certainly don't look real. My advice would be to concentrate on those elements of your life you can change – like your job, where you live, the holidays you choose – and use the money saved from cosmetic surgery to gently indulge yourself in less radical ways.

Q7 Someone said to me recently that you can tell someone's age from behind. It isn't just the way your face looks. I didn't believe them so I walked behind some people yesterday and tried to guess their age. And, nine times

out of ten, I was right. How do I get myself to move or walk like a young person?

Your question reminded me of John Cleese and the Ministry of Silly Walks sketch. The way we walk certainly says something about us. But I wonder if your question is really, 'I don't want to look older.' And the truth is (unless you go down the cosmetic surgery route), 'There ain't nothing you can do about it!' However, as you'll see, you can change how you feel about how you look.

What you asked resonated with something that happened to me recently. I was in a hurry to go out and I put on a pair of old shoes without thinking. Down the years, the shoes have stretched and are now too big for my feet. In order to keep them on, I had to hold my feet in a certain way and found myself thinking that this was how I'll walk when I'm old! And it made me think not about how I looked but how I should look after my feet to ensure they keep on doing a good job.

Your question prompted me to take a look myself the next time I went for a walk to see if you were right and, if so, how it is that people carry themselves differently as they age. I stationed myself outside the shops, the gym and a Pilates studio and played your 'guess the age' game – great fun! I must admit, I'm not sure I agreed with you by the time I'd finished my 'research'. How we walk may be part of it but it's also how we wear our hair, how we hold ourselves and how we dress. There were people who looked older from the front than behind and vice versa.

Last year, a friend of mine was coming out of the tube station when there was a bomb scare, and everyone was being herded along by officials. Those who looked older were being taken off by a different route that involved fewer stairs. She noticed in the crowd a couple she knew being redirected. They'd just come back from taking a group climbing in the Himalayas and were probably fitter than anyone else there but they looked older so had been 'labelled' unfit.

We portray externally what we're feeling inside. I once worked with a young woman with very low self-esteem. She thought she was not as attractive as any of her friends. In reality, she was a good-looking young woman who dressed well. I asked her to walk up and down the corridor in the way she walked in the street. She did so in a despondent manner with her head bent forward and no spring in her step. The message she projected was 'Don't look at me.'

I then asked her to walk in a different way, head held high, a smile on her face, a spring in her step. Immediately, she felt different and said she felt good. I then asked her to walk round the block using her new walk. I knew there were a couple of places she had to pass where she'd be noticed. She came back saying she'd attracted a couple of wolf-whistles. She felt great. Now, I'm not suggesting that we all want to be noticed like that but the message we send out can be in our control.

Our posture and body profile say a lot about us. The way we stand shows others how we view ourselves. Next time you're out, look at the person who stands with their hands on their hips, their shoulders back and their chest puffed out – and, in truth, theyre probably best avoided as they're likely to be spoiling for a fight! Then there's the person who stands with rounded shoulders, head down, looking like a bit of a victim. Or the one with the erect body, head upright and jutting slightly forward, and a macho stance; or the person who, whether sitting or standing, takes up a lot of space – arms on hips and legs wide. Incidentally, notice how much more space most men occupy at meetings than women, who tend to fold into themselves. It's all to do with our body self-image and it's ours to create.

If you want to take control of how you look, you need to consciously make some decisions. Try this exercise.

EXERCISE: TAKING CONTROL

1. Stand in front of the mirror in the way you normally stand.

2. Try several poses: do the aggressive stance, then the victim, the over-confident and the macho.

3. Make yourself look thinner by tightening everything and holding yourself in and now make yourself look fatter by letting it all out.

4. Make a note as you go along of how you feel in each pose. Do any of them make you feel good?

5. Now stand with your feet firmly on the ground, slightly back on your heels, your knees relaxed and your head held high but not protruding. How do you feel? Modify how you stand so you create the pose that makes you feel good and sends out the message you want.

6. Find a place where you can see your back (you'll need two mirrors). Look at your back view. Is it how you think you'd like to be seen from behind? Many of us forget this bit and don't remember that half the world sees us from this angle so it's always worth spending a minute pulling that jumper down or tucking in that shirt!

7. Now you have the perfect stance, practise walking until it feels natural. Know that the message you're giving out is the one you want and, while it may not be that of a young person, well, let's face it, you're not. But it will be the one approved and chosen by you.

Just a word or two on feet before we end. Feet are generally the most neglected part of the body, only noticed when they cause trouble or if you decide to wear unusually high heels. If they're sore (or in the wrong shoes), you won't be able to maintain the posture you want. Rather than hiding them away, treat them to a good pedicure. Then they'll do the job of holding you up so you can present yourself to the world as well as you know how.

Q8 **My son commented the other day on my weight (which has certainly gone up a bit since I started the menopause). He said I used to be slim for my age. I conceded I needed to lose a few pounds but I felt grim, both about my weight and the fact that my son sees weight in relation to age. Is that what happens? Am I just now seen for my age and not for how I look?**

I've noticed how many of the questions I'm asked about how we look seem to involve younger family members. One of the challenges our generation has to face is how best to develop adult-to-adult relationships (see Section 4, Question 1) with our children. I would never have dared pass an unsolicited comment on my mother's size or shape and, if asked, I would be very careful about the answer I gave. Often, if truth be known, I wasn't 100 per cent honest! I think we've come a long way in changing the power in our relationships. I wonder, though, if we've at times gone too far and our children have taken the role of critical parent.

I wonder if our possible overreaction is because we'd never have made an equivalent remark unless we'd really thought our child looked terrible and even then, some of us would have been too inhibited. At times, I think we take the comments of our offspring too seriously and get upset at a deeper level than the remark warrants.

What your son was doing was linking weight to age. In your son's opinion, older people weigh more at different ages. For him, there must be an average weight for a 20-year-old, another for a 40-year-old, another for a 60-year-old and so on. Well, that just isn't true. What I do know is that some of us use this as an excuse along the lines that there's no way we can be thin any more because we're menopausal. My hunch is he hit a raw nerve of yours and verbalised how you see yourself as only an age.

Have you ever been in a situation where you found yourself taking on someone else's thoughts or feelings? For example, your partner comes in from work feeling grumpy and fed up. You can sense it as he closes the front door; the very air seems to change. Prior to this, you'd been feeling fine but you fairly quickly find your mood changing in response to his. In just the same way, I think your son had picked up unconsciously on what you think about yourself and was doing no more than verbalising it, albeit in a less than considerate way.

It's time to change all that – as this exercise is designed to achieve.

EXERCISE: TAKING CONTROL

Take a moment to think of five celebrities over 60 – let's say, Elton John, Terry Wogan, Helen Mirren, Paul McCartney and Honor Blackman. Now consider if the first thing you thought about them was their age. Precisely!

1. How do I want others to see me? Write down five things you want people to notice – for example, a sense of humour, an inner glow, a strong personality, a friendly persona and so on.

2. Observe others who you think project any of these qualities. It is unlikely you will come up with someone who

possesses all these attributes but pick the people who each have one of these particular qualities to the greatest degree. How do they project this quality? Now, try to emulate what they do without attempting to impersonate them. You must adapt the quality that you admire in them and make it your own.

3. Do what it takes to look good. Put in a bit of effort. Lose those extra pounds so you feel good about yourself.

4. Dress (as we discussed earlier) in what suits you. If you have flabby arms, cover them. One great way to reduce the bulges is to buy a body-hugger. We seem to have come full circle and now, instead of the corset, there are some very attractive and cleverly designed pieces of underwear that hold you in all the right places and which only you will know you're wearing. If you feel good, you'll look good.

5. Radiate confidence and happiness. (See Section 3, Question 1.)

It's catching! Good feelings generate good feelings.

None of this will come easily. Like the rest of us, you're going to have to practise. I know it will take a bit of effort but almost certainly not as much as you might imagine.

Nor do I lightly dismiss the weight issue, although it should never become a time-consuming feature of your life. There are many reasons why weight is a problem and a whole host of books have been written on the subject. Our focus here is on the relation of age to weight. So, what is it that makes us worry more at this stage in our lives? Is it because it isn't pretty to have bumps and bulges, or is it because it's unhealthy? Or is it a combination of the two? In other words, does fat equal old?

In my opinion, being fat and unfit is ageing. Fat people move more slowly. They're less agile. They huff and puff when they get out of chairs. They can't run for buses and so on. In no way do they project youthfulness. So, being slim and fit (rather than skinny and drawn) can take years off us. It's not to do with size per se; it's to do with being the right shape and size for your body. And, while it may be a statement of the obvious, it's worth pointing out that carrying excess baggage can lead to conditions such as high blood pressure, diabetes and heart disease, none of which will enhance the quality of your life.

Denial is an arch enemy, although I know it's all too easy to delude ourselves. I have a friend who has ballooned over the years from a size 10 to a size 16. One of her favourite subjects is the quality of fabric nowadays that shrink so quickly; that, and the fact that sizes are so skimpily cut that a modern size 16 is really no more than a 12. She'll tell me this as she happily tucks into a bowl of chips! She could do a lot worse than try the following exercise.

EXERCISE: TRUE CONFESSIONS

1. Choose a time when you're home alone.

2. Take all your clothes off and stand in front of the mirror. Now, jump up and down. What happens? If you're slim and fit, only your breasts will move up and down. If you're not, your tummy will rise and fall, your arms will flap like bat wings, your thighs will roll.

3. Now take a look in the wardrobe. Hand on heart, how many of your clothes are tight? If, like my friend, the answer is most, then – like it or not – you need to address the problem.

4. Finally, get on to the bathroom scales, making sure you stand with both feet firmly in place. (I remember being told once that you could 'lose' pounds by weighing yourself first thing in the morning after having been to the loo and breathing out three long breaths before climbing on to the scales v-e-r-y slowly and standing with one foot just resting on the surface. It took me a long time to work out that that might help the first time you tried it but, after that, the comparison was going to be the same on each occasion.)

Having honestly undertaken this test, you should now be in no doubt about exactly where the problem lies. Are you overweight, or is it that your shape has changed down the years? Both can be rectified. As Dr Miriam Stoppard points out in her book *Defying Age*, 'Eat more, weigh less is the secret of a longer life.' If you can get your weight to where it is healthy for your height, and your head to an understanding of how lovely you are, you won't even notice the next time anyone makes a critical comment for the simple reason that there won't be a next time!

❦ Section Three ❦

You're Never Too Old to…
Get Laid

I t often strikes me when I'm out and about how many 50+ couples walk hand-in-hand down the street and how it isn't only the young who are demonstrative in public. Sadly, that still isn't as true when it comes to gay relationships. I do hope that our generation can help bring about a shift in the social climate so that our children will be freer and more open with their sexuality, whatever it may be. Having said that, trying to embark on a new relationship – no matter your sexuality – is never a pushover.

Q1 My husband of 40 years has just left me for a younger woman. He told me I had become boring and sexless. How will I ever pick myself up off the floor? I feel old, fat, tired and useless.

The important thing now is not a discussion of what a louse he's been: it's what you're going to do next. It seems to me that you have a choice: either you can fall victim to your situation or you can try to make something good out of something bad. The latter might strike you as impossible at the moment but, with time, things will change and you will heal.

I'm aware that there are a lot of practical issues that you'll have to consider but I'm also pretty certain you don't want advice on how to handle your finances. This is to do with regaining your confidence and once again becoming the amazing person you are. Once that's done, the rest will fall into place.

Your feelings of self-worth have taken a hard knock. We all have times when something happens that knocks us sideways. We stop feeling attractive, useful, fun, interesting and valuable, and suddenly imagine we're all the opposites. Then we begin to project on to others what we feel about ourselves, setting up a cycle of depressing and debilitating feelings. In the end, our friends get fed up with us, too. Your question suggests that you think your feelings of self-worth belong to your husband and not to you, that what he says is right. As you've been married for 40 years, I don't suppose you think he's been right all the time, so why think so now?

It's time to take stock of yourself but, just before you do, let me explain about filters. We each perceive the world from our own viewpoint. We understand the world through our senses – our eyes, ears, touch, taste and smell. We build on our unique beliefs, values and attitudes through our interpretation of our experiences. We establish a unique set of filters based on these and we interpret the world through these filters. We therefore all see the world differently from our own viewpoint.

Your husband is seeing you through his unique set of filters, which are coloured by his experiences, fears, beliefs, fantasies and so on. What he says is not the truth! If you take his filter to be the truth, you will be seeing yourself through the wrong eyes.

So now take a moment to think through these questions:

- How do I see myself now?

- How would my closest friend/children/work colleagues describe me? If you don't know, ask them and, if two or more people agree, it's more than likely to be the truth.

- What's stopping me from feeling all right about myself?

- What's it doing for me feeling like this?

- How would I like to feel?

- What three things would I like to do that would make me feel good?

OK, now you know what you want, you've completed the first and most important step. You've created a plan! You've had a knock, your confidence has taken a nose-dive. These confidence-building exercises should take you to the next stage.

EXERCISE: RING OF CONFIDENCE

Stage 1

1. Think of a situation in which you feel totally self-confident and answer the following questions:

   - What is that situation?

   - What do you say to yourself in that situation?

   - How do you feel?

   - How do you behave as a consequence?

2. Now think of a current situation in which you experience a lack of self-worth and ask yourself exactly the same questions. Having done that, ask yourself these questions:

   - What could I say to myself that's positive?

   - How could I feel differently?

   - What direct action could I take? (For example, if you want to feel more relaxed, you could breathe more deeply.)

   Now, having looked at the situation and come up with something, you need to make it feel real.

Stage 2

1. Draw an imaginary circle on the floor in front of you. This is a magic circle. You can only be confident and excellent in here.

2. Stand outside it and think of a time when you were confident. It can be the example you used before or something else. It can be something small like driving your car to the supermarket or large like giving a speech to a hundred people. When you've got it, step into the circle and associate into the event, i.e. relive it. (See Section 1, Question 3 for the technique.)

- See what you see

- Hear what you hear

- Feel what you feel

- Hold your body as you do when confident

- Breathe as you breathe when feeling good

- Really get that feeling

3. Now come out of your circle, stepping backwards. Think of a second time when you were really confident. When you have it, climb back into the circle and associate into the event.

Do this twice more so you can put on confidence like you can your overcoat!

4. Now think of something you have to do where you don't feel confident, for example, going to a family function without your husband. Climb into the magic circle. Remember, you can only be confident in here. So put on that confidence coat.

- See what you see going well

- Hear what you hear sounding good

- Hold yourself as a woman with everything going for her

- Breathe with a sense of serenity

5. When you really feel in charge, imagine yourself exiting forward from the circle cloaked in that ring of confidence.

It sounds simple and it is. Our physiology runs us. (See Section 6, Question 5 on managing stress.) We create hormones (e.g. adrenalin) when we're threatened by a situation and these relay a message that our brain interprets as panic and danger. Our bodies get ready to cope with whatever it is and we feel bad. Send a message that all is right in our world and the hormones respond accordingly. You may need to practise a few times but the more you do, the more confident you'll feel.

It's worth repeating that behaviour breeds behaviour. If you exude confidence, the other person will feel confident in you and in themselves. I take my confidence circle with me in my handbag and bring it out when needed. Sometimes, if I find myself going wobbly, I pop to the loo and get it out. Within minutes, I'm feeling like a million dollars.

What's so important is that you take your power back and don't let what he thinks prevent you doing what makes you feel good.

Q2 **I have been on my own for the last five years following a rather messy divorce. I think I'm now ready to meet someone new. But I haven't a clue how to go about it.**

I wonder if it's strictly true that you really don't have a clue – or is it perhaps that you're just a bit rusty? It's certainly a fact that, if we don't use a skill for a bit, we forget how to do these things. The skill of dating is much like riding a bike when you first get on it after a long break. Invariably, you'll be a bit wobbly at first and then, within a minute or two, you'll be riding as proficiently as you did 20 years earlier.

Right, now take a few minutes to think about what you did when you were young and looking for potentially meaningful relationships. The great thing is that this time you're approaching the prospect with all the wisdom and knowledge of a mature and experienced woman, someone so much better equipped than the last time around.

One of the main factors that stops us from going out and getting what we want is the negative thought patterns we have. It's the inner self talking: I'm too old/fat/inexperienced/I don't want to be hurt again like I was last time/I'm frightened of being rejected/I couldn't bear to lose again/Nobody sticks around for ever/Nobody will fancy me/I'm not as attractive or sexy as I might have been . . . and so on and so forth. Well, believe me, with all that going on in your head, you don't stand the remotest chance of being appealing!

In Section 1, Question 3, we addressed negative thinking. If you need a reminder, go back and try both the exercises again. Now, you are ready to think about meeting someone new. You could try a dating agency, answering or placing an 'ad', going on the internet or going in person to somewhere you believe people with similar interests and aspirations might go.

I once coached a single woman who was increasingly distressed that she never met anyone. She said she was out nearly every night so couldn't understand why she didn't meet like-minded people. So we examined her week. Two nights a week, she met women friends who were in the same position and they talked about their lack of success when it came to meeting potential partners or others with similar interests. Once a week, she went to supper with different couples who never invited anyone else as they both enjoyed her company so much that they didn't want to share her with anyone else (or so she maintained, although I wondered if they'd have kept her away from their other friends if she'd had a partner). Another night, she spent with her parents. Twice a week, she stayed in to prepare for work the next day, do the chores and have some downtime. And, on the seventh day, rather than resting, she'd go to the theatre, a film or concert with one of her unattached friends and then out for a meal.

Busy she was. She was not, however doing anything that enabled her to meet anyone new. And yet, it never occurred to her that she was self-sabotaging!

Within a week of our meeting, she had reordered her time. She retained her evening with her parents and the two nights she kept aside for herself. She reduced the women friends to one night. She stopped going to her 'couples' friends on her own, and asked them to invite her with other friends. Even if they didn't know an eligible person, their friends might and that opened up the pool. She joined a new tennis club – a passion of hers – and went on her own so she had to meet new people.

She also set up a private dinner club with a select group of women friends who all loved cooking and entertaining. Once a month, one of them hosted a dinner party, each woman being obliged to bring a potential partner/lover. This was a particularly successful ploy since the core members of the group knew each other so well and had so many interests in common and so did their friends.

In the event, and within the first year, four out of the original six met people with whom they had relationships. And, as they each paired off, another woman was invited to take their place.

One thing of which I'm certain is that, if you go to events, clubs or any meetings with a friend and stand talking to them all evening, you're much less likely to meet anyone new. One person on their own looks much more appealing because you're sending out the signal that you'd welcome some company.

Choose places to go – talks, clubs, societies, singles' holidays, evening classes – where you know it's more likely you'll meet someone who has similar interests to yours.

EXERCISE: PLANNING YOUR LEISURE TIME

If you're keen to consider the possibility of a new relationship, try this simple exercise:

1. Look at your week. How do you spend your leisure time?

2. What percentage of your leisure time is spent on activities that get in the way of your meeting new people?

3. What could you do to change your week to give yourself space to meet someone new? I can guarantee they won't come knocking at your front door for that express purpose!

4. Decide on one activity you'll take up each week to increase your chances of meeting a new partner/lover.

Remember that everyone you meet will have at least one friend who you don't know. By extending your circle, you'll find you have both a more interesting time socially and you'll put yourself into a place where you're much more likely to meet someone new. And one guaranteed way of breaking the ice is to talk to other people about how hard it is to meet anyone new!

If taking yourself to somewhere new on your own seems daunting, there are lots of ways nowadays to meet people – initially, at least – without leaving home. But this will take time and planning so be sure to make space for it in a busy schedule. The personal ads in newspapers, professional journals and magazines are used by thousands of people looking for a relationship. Internet websites are international so the world is at your fingertips, and an astonishing number of people use these sites, some of which are especially geared to particular professions, interests and age groups.

According to research carried out in 2005 by Dr Jeff Gavin of the University of Bath, 6 million Britons signed up to internet dating sites, a figure supported by UK dating sites who claim that meeting people online is now a very popular and mainstream way to find a date. Dr Gavin's research suggests that internet dating is proving a much more successful way of finding long-term romance and friendship for thousands of people than was previously thought. His survey of 229 people aged between 18 and 65 who have used UK internet dating sites found that, when couples who had built up a significant relationship by emailing or chatting online met for the first time, 94 per cent went on to see each other again.

And it's popular with the over-fifties, too. Nearly a quarter of US subscribers of www.match.com, an internationally successful internet dating site, are 50+, more than double the number in 2005. Yahoo Personals, meanwhile, has seen double-digit growth in the number of users over 50 in 2005–7. An article published in the February 2006 issue of *Newsweek* magazine emphasised the specialisation of internet dating sites available to the over-fifties in the US. Online agencies such as SciConnect.com, a specialist agency for science professionals mainly in the US and Canada, says that more than 60 per cent of its members are between 40 and 59. Baby boomers searching for same-age partners can comb through sites like www.perfectmatch.com (63 per cent are 35 to 60) and www.primesingles.net, a 50+ site whose membership grew 39 per cent in 2005.

One big change is that, less than forty years ago, most people who were on their own were either widowed and expected to remain alone for the rest of their lives or were women who had never married and who felt love had passed them by. But all that has changed. Today, with as many as one in three marriages ending in divorce and others who have yet to find their soul partner, there are a lot of people looking for a relationship. If you're 50 and healthy, there's certainly no reason to give up. Given current life expectancy, there's no reason why you couldn't enjoy thirty or more years of a fulfilling relationship.

If using the internet or personal ads in search of your potential partner, it's worth taking a moment to consider precisely what it is that you're looking for. This exercise may help.

EXERCISE: PICTURE THIS

First, write a list of qualities and attributes you would like to find in your ideal partner, such as:

- What would they look like?

- What would be the values by which you'd hope they ran their lives?

- What kind of job would they do?

- What kind of financial position would they be in?

- Are you looking for someone ordered or spontaneous?

- Would you mind whether or not they had children?

- What leisure pursuits would you like them to enjoy?

  1. Having now created the ideal partner in your mind's eye, ask yourself the following question. Is this ideal just like all the other relationships you've had? If so, are you liable to make similar mistakes? Modify your picture and set your sights at the right sort of person.

  2. Don't be too choosy, particularly when it comes to appearance. So, you've always gone for brown hair or blue eyes? Don't close your mind to a green-eyed blond. Financial security, however, if that's what's important to you, is another matter. Don't go for someone who's laissez-faire when it comes to money. It will only lead to upsets.

  3. Decide what kind of relationship you want. Are you looking for someone to go on dates with? A friend or a lover? Someone to live with or someone to marry?

  4. Once you've honestly worked out what it is you're looking for, decide where you're going to place the advert. If you want someone with left-wing leanings, of course you don't put it in a right-wing publication and so on.

Q3 **I have been on my own for a while. I have just met a new potential lover. I am 52 and my figure isn't what it used to be. Even when I stand up very straight and hold myself in, I can still see lots of sagging bits! How will I**

**ever feel confident enough to take my clothes off even if we
are in the dark? Just thinking about it makes me feel anything
but sexy . . .**

How lovely to have met someone new. That must be very exciting.
But it sounds as though you're also feeling a bit daunted. It's
funny how we want something and often fantasise about how
good it will be and then do a fantastic sabotage job on ourselves
to spoil it. I wonder if he, too, is worrying about taking his clothes
off. More probably, he's thanking his lucky stars that he's met
someone so gorgeous.

As a general rule, women are much more anxious about the way
they look than most men. Instead of taking a leaf out of his book
and telling yourself how great that you're attracted to a real hunk
who seems to feel the same way, you torture yourself with
thoughts of how unprepossessing you'll look in the altogether.

It's hard at times to feel sexy and attractive at any age and
certainly harder as we get older. We're surrounded by pictures
of beautiful young things in glossy magazines. The pictures we
see of older women are of celebrities, many of whom owe their
looks to artful photography, clever make-up and the cosmetic
surgeon's knife.

You say it's been a while since you've been in this position so
you may have forgotten what it is that makes you feel sexy. So
let's start by focusing on that. Find somewhere quiet to sit and
where you won't be disturbed. Now try the following exercise.

EXERCISE: WHATEVER TURNS YOU ON

I. Take a moment to think about these questions:

- When have you felt really sexy?

- What was happening in your life at that time?

- What made you feel sexy?

- Do you feel sexy as often these days?

- When did you feel best about your body?

- Was it when you were young, or have there been times later in life when, despite having older skin, you felt happier in it?

- What turns you on now (besides your new potential lover!)?

2. Draw a timeline to represent your relationships. This line will represent your life in relationship/sexuality terms. Start when you were first aware you were a boy or girl – or when you first fancied a boy or girl in the playground. The example below is just there to trigger your thinking.

Example Timeline

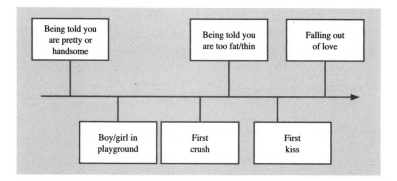

Now complete your own timeline:

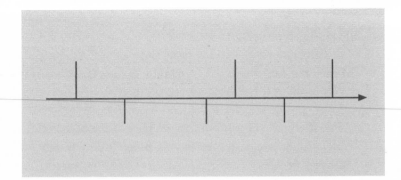

3. Plot your confidence in your sexiness, on a scale of 0–10
   (with 10 being very confident) at each event on the scale
   on the graph.

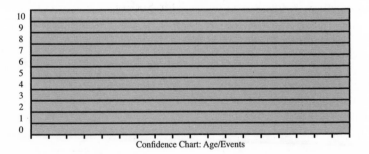

Confidence Chart: Age/Events

Take a look at your timeline and consider whether confidence
in your sexiness is actually related to your age and body shape
or to other things. For many of us, it isn't necessarily age-
specific. This is, therefore, another myth you can throw out of
the window.

I expect you've discovered that, if you're going to feel sexy, you
need to feel good about yourself. It is really important to identify

all the ingredients that help you feel good (as well as those that make you feel bad).

4. Fill in the chart below:

Makes me feel good	Makes me feel bad

Now you have that list, make sure that you've got in place all the things you need to feel fantastic. Some of us feel sexy when we're wearing sexy underwear, and it isn't just the young who can wear confidence-boosting lingerie. There are some lingerie companies in the Resource List for Section 3 that specifically cater for the more mature woman.

As I explain in Section 6, Question 2, if we think negative thoughts we create negativity around us which becomes a self-fulfilling prophecy. Every time you start going into a negative spiral, train yourself to focus on what makes you feel good, not on what makes you feel bad.

Let's go back to taking your clothes off. You're by no means alone in thinking this. I once had a client who talked about the first time she had sex with her new partner. It was after a party. Passion was running high so she didn't even have time to stop and think about what she might look like naked. The next morning, she woke up wanting to go to the loo and found herself frozen to the bed. How would she ever get up? She kept hoping that he'd get up first. Her wait was rewarded and he happily bounced out of bed.

It was only when she took an objective look at him did she see a middle-aged man with a paunch and balding head. But none of it mattered: she still felt turned on by him. It was something of a revelation to her when she realised that, similarly, he wouldn't see her drooping breasts and flabby tummy but a woman he fancied. Just in case you aren't convinced, remember the old trick of keeping a towel by the bed to wrap yourself in in the morning, although, if you're in the grip of passion, those sort of details tend to get forgotten!

Now let's consider how you maintain your sexy feelings once you've taken your clothes off. How we feel about our looks (see Section 2, Question 1) is so closely linked to our emotions and the resulting message we send out to the other person, it's very important to stay in touch with our feelings. A tense or sulky woman is no turn-on. It's also a sure way of losing that sexy feeling. A good exercise to do if you start feeling tense is to squeeze your eyebrows with your thumb and forefinger. Start at the bridge of your nose and move outwards. Then press your thumb and forefinger into your cheekbones and hold them there for a few seconds. This releases tension in your face and boosts circulation.

If you know you're likely to have sex that evening, make sure you're wearing underwear you like. Do what you feel makes your body feel nice. For some women, getting rid of hairy legs and armpits is important; for others, it's a pedicure or a good haircut. Spend a bit of time pampering yourself. Treat yourself to a body massage – it'll make you feel stimulated and vibrant. Eat foods that release serotonin into the brain. Fish and white meat like turkey and chicken are mood-boosting foods that produce serotonin. Foods high in vitamin B, such as bananas and avocados, can be beneficial to your mood as they convert an amino acid called tryptophan into serotonin. This is a natural 'happy' hormone and, the more that circulates around your body, the better you'll feel.

Choose where you want to have this first encounter. Make the place sexy. For example, have nice music playing and release sensuous scents such as jasmine and sandalwood via candles: a great way to stimulate sensual feelings. I think you're in for a fab time!

Q4 **I find the company of my husband boring. He's always watching TV and we never talk; he falls asleep with the TV control in his hand. The thought of spending the rest of my life like this is more than worrying. Up till now, it hasn't mattered so much as I have a very busy job and have to take quite a lot of work home. But retirement is looming and then what?**

There are lots of things you don't reveal in your question. For example, have you passively put up with this situation for years, or have you discussed it in detail with your husband? I'm going to make the assumption that up to now you haven't said anything. Well, if I may be so bold, you've undoubtedly contributed to the problem. You say you've been absorbed in your job, day and night. Is it possible that your accommodating husband decided that, rather than disturb you, he'd while away his time in front of the box?

Whatever the reason, you and he have got into a rather dull place where the relationship isn't doing much for either of you and it needs a bit of a boost. (Several of the questions in this book explore different aspects of relationship-boosting so do take a look at them.)

I want to explain a psychological model to you that I think will help illustrate what might be going on. Called the OK Corral, it comes from a theory called Transactional Analysis and sets out possible patterns of communication:

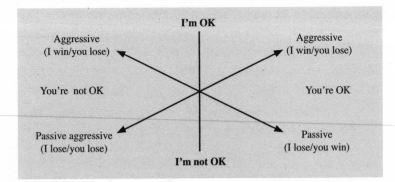

© Franklin H. Ernst, 1971

When we arrive in the world, and unless there has been a specific birth trauma, we are at peace with ourselves and with others. We're likely to perceive the world from the perspective of: 'I'm OK, you're OK.' This doesn't mean we think we're marvellous or any better than anyone else; just that we have no reason to believe anything negative will happen. We then all start experiencing life and trying to make sense of it. However idyllic your childhood, there will always be things that don't go perfectly to plan.

Being new to the world, children have limited resources and experiences on which to draw. This can be explained by this model. For example, if someone was treated punitively, talked down to and not made to feel secure as a child, they may begin to believe 'I'm not an OK person but you are.' This might be the only sense they can make of their experiences. If, however, they were picked on and bullied as a child, they may have learnt that the only way to survive was to bully others. This may have made them feel stronger and in control. And they may believe 'I'm OK but you're not.'

Others may have had the experience where they know the other person is being unpleasant but, because of their lack of self-esteem, don't have the confidence to deal with the situation. These people are likely to believe 'I'm not OK and nor are you.'

But these are just our perceptions of the world; they're not facts. Concentrate on feeling OK about yourself. That way lies respect, confidence and self-belief.

Now let's go back to your question. You can tackle your problem in a number of ways:

Passive – he's doing what he likes. I'm not very interesting anyway so why would he want to chat to me? I'll just watch telly, too, when I finish my work even though it doesn't interest me.

Passive aggressive/manipulative – I don't think he'll listen to me but I also don't think he'll change so why bother? But I'm certainly not going to let him have an easy ride.

Aggressive – I'm right and he's wrong. He's dull and boring and I'm going to tell him in no uncertain terms!

Assertive – I truly believe we're both doing the best we can even if this isn't the best patch in our marriage. So I'm going to talk to him and discuss what we both want out of our relationship. And I promise to listen to what he has to say.

That's easier said than done. One of the hardest things to do is to really listen to people, especially when we're fed up with them. But, if you're going to improve your relationship, it's essential you let your husband have his say. Listening involves being able to put yourself in the other person's shoes in order to 'hear' and interpret both what they're saying and what they're not saying. The great skill in communication is the ability to put oneself in another's shoes, understanding the music behind the words.

Effective listening means being able to understand what the other person is saying in the way they want it to be understood. In order to do this, you have to *want* to understand the other person's point of view. In fact, you may well find that, if you listen carefully enough, the other person will end up making your point for you.

It's worth considering some of the things that distract and block us from listening properly:

- We think we know what the other person will say.

- We pre-judge what they're about to say.

- Our minds wander on to a different topic.

- We're preoccupied with working out our next response.

- We think ahead to the implications of what is being said and what it might mean for us.

- We don't like the speaker at that minute and are irritated by the speaker's appearance or mannerisms.

Here's how to overcome the obvious pitfalls:

1. Avoid distractions. Concentrate on the other person. Watch their expressions and movements. Ignore ringing telephones. Don't do something else, like preparing the supper, at the same time.

2. Don't assume. You'll never really understand what the other person is saying if you make assumptions. You'll only reinforce what you thought you knew already. Or, as someone once said, 'Don't assume: it makes an ASS of U and ME.'

3. Don't interrupt. Let the other person have their say – even if you disagree.

4. Stop talking! Nature gave you two ears and one tongue.
   Take the hint.

5. Ask questions. The only way you can check your
   understanding is by finding out more.

6. Summarise throughout the conversation so you're both
   clear where you've got to in your discussion.

Just a word on questions. Some questions close down the conversation or lead the person to the questioner's conclusions. Others open up the conversation and illuminate. These are known as open questions and will indicate to the person being asked that you're interested and following rather than trying to steer them to your own conclusions. Open questions start with Who, Why, What, Which, When, Where and How.

You may be thinking, 'Why should I do all the work? Why should I be the one to try and make it better?' Well, as they say, it takes two to tango so why not you? If you start to really talk to each other I think you'll stop being bored and reconnect in the way you did once upon a time.

Q5 I have recently become aware that I'm attracted to women and not to men. This is the first time in my life that I've wanted a same-sex relationship. I am 57, divorced, with nearly grown-up children and a close, extended family. I don't know who to turn to to discuss this. Am I mad? Is this normal? Who can I tell? Can I be open about this? What will the children and family think? Will they still want to know me? Where would I meet someone?

You raise a lot of questions, understandably enough as you're facing something so new and unfamiliar. But your anxiety may not be as unusual as you might think. I'm sure you're feeling out on a limb but some of your questions are ones asked by men and women whatever their sexuality – for example, 'Where would I meet someone?' Well, if you're not in a relationship and want one, it's important that you go to the best places to achieve your goal, as it would be for anyone hoping to meet a new partner. (See Section 3, Question 2.)

And no, you're not mad. I'd say you're probably as normal as the rest of us. Having feelings for someone of the same sex is much more common than you might think and that can occur at different points in our lives. Current government figures suggest that between 5 and 7 per cent of the UK population is lesbian, gay or bisexual. In the twenty-first century, it would be sad to think that the idea of exploring same-sex relationships, even if only in your mind, could make you a social outcast.

Now let's take a look at this possible change in your sexual preference and see what has actually happened. Does changing your sexuality mean that all of you has changed? From your question, it sounds as though you have a real fear that your friends and family – and perhaps especially your children – won't want to relate to you as they will no longer see you for who you are but just as an unknown gay woman. Does sound a bit barmy put like that, doesn't it? The more we understand ourselves, the easier it is for us to manage our fears and find a solution, so take a few minutes to do this exercise.

EXERCISE: WHAT MATTERS MOST?

I. Below is a list of qualities and attributes, some of which will be important to you. It's not comprehensive so you may want to add some of your own. Circle the ten that are the most important:

Honesty, Integrity, Humour, Sincerity, Happiness, Passion, Power, Acceptance, Kindness, Independence, Freedom, Love, Joy, Hope, Peace, Wealth, Success, a Spirit of Adventure, Respect, Trust, Understanding, Compassion, Resilience, Courtesy, Having a Family, Variety, Religion, Reputation, Inner Harmony, Community Spirit, Competence, Influence, Beauty, Competition, an Awareness of the Environment, Knowledge, Security, Equality, Self-reliance, Inner Strength, Leadership, Punctuality, Loyalty, Friendship, Growth, Development, Privacy, Fame, Justice, Innovation, Wisdom, Reliability.

2. For each value, ask yourself the following questions:

    • What does it mean to me?

    • Why is it important to me?

    • What does it say about me?

    • How does it manifest itself in my daily life?

3. Now prioritise your top ten values.

4. Imagine yourself in a same-sex relationship. Do these values still hold?

If, as I suspect, the answer is yes, then nothing that really matters to you and guides your life has changed. Our values and beliefs are what make us who we are. They are the foundation stones that affect the way we behave, live and relate to other people.

For example, if honesty is high on your list and you don't think you can be honest with your friends and family about how you want to live your life, you'll find yourself stressed by having to live a lie. You'll forever be torn between your inner needs and desires and your actions. Learning how to live by our beliefs and values is essential. Lots of our conflicting beliefs are ingrained in us when we are small. They are learnt from our families and our childhood influences. If you have conflicting beliefs, take a look at Section 5, Question 4, on creating positive beliefs.

Having identified that nothing fundamental about you changes if your sexual preference alters, we need to look at how to tackle the loved ones you fear you might lose. If your children were asked to write a speech about you, what are the ten attributes they would say best describe you? Do the same now for a close friend and a parent/sibling. I don't suppose your sexuality would appear on anyone's list.

So what are you worried about? If we asked anyone who is fond of you what their hopes for you were over the next 30 years, what would they say? I'm pretty certain it would be along the lines that they hoped you'd be happy, fulfilled, healthy and active. If that's the case, your only problem is your unfounded fear.

I realise that this might be a tricky and difficult conversation. We often worry that our children will have very conservative views about how parents should behave. Doing something different is, in their mind, the prerogative of the young! It is of course possible that your children may react negatively to your revelation and it may be a slow process convincing them that nothing has changed except for who you now fancy. Most young people are overly concerned about what others think and want to be just like their friends. While that may be understandable, why should it be any of their business? I don't suppose they showed any interest in your sex life up until this point!

Either way, you're certainly not the first or last woman to be faced with this dilemma. There are some really helpful organisations and websites where you can discuss this further and lots of written resources. See the Bibliography and Resource List to this section.

I also can't help wondering if you are perhaps projecting some of your own anxieties on to others. It's really important that you should be comfortable with who you are – or, to use the jargon, that you should own what is yours – so that you can be clear when talking to family and friends. But no one's blaming you for having conflicting thoughts and feelings. You're about to embark on a journey into the unknown. I'm not for one minute wanting to dismiss your anxieties. I'm only too well aware that the world is full of prejudiced people who believe they're right. And I have personal experience of people who have 'come out' to their families with the assurance in advance that there is no revelation that will be unacceptable to them – but they went off the deep end when they were told about the person's sexuality.

So, you'll have to make a considered decision as to who you trust and who you don't. Sadly, sometimes people become irrational when their beliefs are challenged and they may attack rather than support. Keep in mind who might be rattled by your revelation and try to ensure that you share your innermost thoughts with people you know will be cool about it and encourage you on the next stage of your journey. Some estimates suggest that perhaps as many as one in ten of us is not exclusively heterosexual so you're not alone in the world, even if it feels like it at the minute. For all you know, one of your children may be worrying about the same thing and wondering how to tell their mother.

Learning how to have sex with another woman will be different and something that will undoubtedly make you anxious in advance. If you think back to your first sexual experience, you were probably pretty concerned, so being a 'virgin' all over again will be almost as scary. There are numerous books on the subject, see this section's Resource List. Finding a sensitive lover who understands that this is a first for you would be a good way to learn the techniques, if you're fortunate enough. If it becomes a lifestyle decision and you want to bring your same-sex relationship out into the open, then use the support of your lover to help you through the possible, although not inevitable, negative reactions. At all times, stay true to who you are as a person and you can't go wrong. Good luck.

Q6 **I'm going through the menopause and I don't think my body any longer works in the way it once did. I've lost interest in sex. I'm no longer aroused by my partner. In truth, I never find myself sexually stimulated. I know that my partner still wants to have sex. I find myself making excuses to avoid rejecting him by going to bed early or pretending to be asleep. Now I worry he'll go for a younger model. What can I do? And how do I rekindle my interest in sex?**

There has been lots written about the physical changes that occur during the menopause so I'm just going to touch on this briefly here. In the Bibliography, there are a number of books you can read for more information as well as some useful websites in the Resource List. The most common effects which can last a while, several years for some, are due to the reduction in the amount of oestrogen your body produces and this can lead to hot flushes, night sweats, tiredness, irritability, mood swings, clumsiness, memory problems, dry vagina, loss of sex drive, urinary problems and decrease in bone density.

A list like that sounds pretty scary, doesn't it? The reality is that many women don't get any symptoms while they're going through the menopause and only a few really suffer with the most common symptoms. But, if you are suffering, it's well worth going to your GP or a Well Woman clinic.

There are lots of ways to alleviate any symptoms. HRT can be a great help to some women but it doesn't suit everyone; there is also some concern that it could have serious side-effects such as increasing the risk of breast cancer and of developing a deep-vein thrombosis. It is really important that you discuss this with your doctor as you might not want to expose yourself to any risk, and for some, due to their's or their family's medical history, it is not advisable. There are herbal alternatives such as phyto-oestrogens, black cohosh, evening primrose and other prepara-tions that can be taken and any number of complementary therapies including acupuncture, yoga, aromatherapy and reflex-ology that have produced amazing results for some in reducing menopausal symptoms. Gentle exercise and relaxation techniques are also invaluable.

If you're having health problems during the menopause, you're bound to feel below par and less sexy, so finding ways to improve your health is important. Exercise can be a great help as, every time you exercise, your body converts other hormones into a form of oestrogen called oestrone and the more oestrogen your body produces, the younger you'll feel. This is something worth remembering long after the menopause is over.

Different experts have different views on how the menopause affects our libido. Some say that women feel more liberated and relaxed as a result of not having to worry about getting pregnant, while others blame the physical side-effects of the menopause for reduced libido and enjoyment of sex. You should also note that other life events – worry over elderly relatives and/or teenage children, and pressures from work – may often coincide with the onset of the menopause and could contribute towards putting you off sex.

I don't want to dismiss the effect of the physical symptoms on you but I recommend a look at what is going on in your head. The brain is the most powerful sexual organ in our body. The hypothalamus responds to sexual stimulation and the cerebral cortex allows us to have sexy thoughts. If that isn't stimulated, you won't feel sexy.

For some of us, our feelings are coloured by the societal view that women aren't sexy over a certain age. It's almost as though we're doing something that isn't very nice. A friend of mine reported that her sister said that the thought of older women getting laid slightly turned her stomach; that, she felt, was the province of the young. I'd like to bet she'll revise her views when she hits 50 or 60!

In order to feel sexy, we have to feel comfortable in our bodies. If we look in the mirror and see something we don't like, such as rolls of fat or a wrinkled face, the last thing we want is someone looking at us and touching us. So, looking after your appearance is essential if you're going to feel sexy. This is the same for your partner; if they're sagging all over the place or have a large paunch, it may just not do it for you.

But there's nothing to say that passion dwindles as we age. Ask yourself if you still get turned on when you look at someone in the street or fantasise about Brad Pitt or George Clooney up there on the cinema screen. Talking to women who are thinking about or who've started new relationships in their fifties and sixties, it's clear to me that they certainly haven't lost their libido. The mistake we make, though, is in imagining that lovemaking will be the same as when we first discovered the joys of sex. As we get older, some of us may look for loving in a different way and not necessarily want to express ourselves sexually.

What you raise here are two issues: one is that you've gone off sex (assuming the menopause is to blame) and the other is that your partner and you are out of sync and that has made you anxious. I'm sure you've been through phases before when he may have wanted more sex than you or vice versa and, if he didn't run off then, there's no reason why it'll happen now. If you're anxious, it'll sap your energy and, if you want to revitalise your sex life, it's good to keep fit – both physically and mentally.

There are things you can do to help to increase your libido apart from creating a warm and sexy environment. Try suggesting taking a shower or bath together or massaging each other with sweet-smelling oils. Try making love somewhere different in the house or at a different time, always ensuring you have enough time to touch and stroke each other first rather than rushing headlong towards orgasm. Talking of orgasms, don't make that your goal. It's fine just to enjoy each other's bodies. You don't have to have intercourse to feel intimate.

There are other things you can do on your own to arouse sexual feelings. Indulge in daydreams about sex. Find a nice private place to be where you won't be disturbed and just let your mind wander; create or read some sexual fantasies and see how your body reacts. Masturbation is also a good way to stimulate yourself so you begin to rediscover those feelings within you. If you have a fear that sex will be painful because you are less lubricated than you used to be, see if that's true when you masturbate. If it is, go and talk to your GP and ask for some lubricant.

I wonder if part of the problem is that you haven't given yourself permission to be sexy now you're older. Let me give you some facts from a federally funded survey undertaken by the University of Chicago (and published in the *New England Journal of Medicine*, 2007). Less than 30 per cent of people in their sixties and seventies think their sex drive has reduced. Many report that throughout their lives there have been times when sex wasn't on their mind because of other things happening that affected their energy levels and moods. But it wasn't to do with their age. Many said that sex is the same as it was when they were younger and a third said it is better now they're older. The frequency of sexual activity remained much the same for people until they were well into their late seventies. There are a lot of years when you could miss out on one of life's pleasures unless you look at how to shift this feeling of yours. One way to help you to come up with a solution might be to think back to a time in your life when your sex drive was low. How did you overcome it then? See if you can use that strategy now. (See Question 3 in this section on feeling good.)

Another very good way to break the logjam is to talk to your partner. Don't start the conversation when he's wanting sex and you don't. Choose a different time in a different place. Discuss possible solutions. Ask him to tell you how he sees you and what it is that he finds sexy about you. Talk to him about your feelings, your worries. Be brave enough to discuss techniques. Maybe something he does while making love to you no longer appeals. Say as much. Equally, there's nothing worse than finding you can't get into a position you used to because your body has become less supple.

And never forget to laugh if things don't quite go according to plan. Good sex is all about having good fun.

Q7 **For the last 22 years, I've been on holiday with my husband and all or some of our children. This year, it will be just the two of us. We've booked two weeks on a Greek island because we like the sun and that's the type of holiday we usually have. How am I going to manage two weeks alone with him? What are we going to talk**

about? Don't think I don't like him. I do. But I'm just concerned that we're out of the habit of being alone together.

This is such a common question so don't feel you're on your own. I know family and jobs can be all-consuming but it never ceases to amaze me that we forget to really talk to our nearest and dearest, to maintain our own special relationship. Of course, in some ways, we don't ever really stop talking to them. We talk about the children, the teacher who's upsetting them, their exams, health, our jobs, finances, mortgages, household issues and extended family and friends.

What we fail to talk about is us, about who we are. It's as though we're suspended somewhere in outer space unable to be reached and then, when there's eventually some time to talk to each other about our feelings, we're stuck. Down the long years when we're preoccupied with raising a family and holding down a job, we dream of those days when it'll just be the two of us. The time arrives and those skills seem to have rusted over.

All is not lost. Cast your mind back to when you were young and on holiday. Think of the three things that dominated your holidays. I bet it was sex, food and lying in the sun. It certainly wasn't talking about your feelings. So is it the art of talking you've lost? Or is it relating to each other physically and emotionally?

You say you like your husband, which is a great start, so let's concentrate on getting you back together as a couple and not as Mum and Dad. It seems an obvious question but I wonder if you've talked to him about this. Are you assuming that he's looking forward to two scintillating weeks of your dazzling repartee? No, I didn't think so! In truth, he's probably thinking much the same as you.

First thing then is to sit down and tell him your concerns. It may be a bit of an uncomfortable conversation as you'll both have to confront your anxieties but it'll certainly lead you to a much better place. And there are ways to have these sorts of conversations.

- Choose a moment when you have plenty of time.

- Check that neither of you has a pressing business engagement.

- Wait for a day when neither of you is feeling stressed.

- Sit down with a cup of tea or glass of wine and agree to take half an hour to plan the holiday.

- Don't start by telling him why you're worried. Begin by pointing out that going on holiday together alone, without the children, is going to be a new experience for both of you.

- Tell him you want to enjoy it and him to enjoy it, too. Explain that, as you've both been so fixated by your children, you've probably forgotten what each of you likes doing.

- What does he want to do on holiday? Both of you make a list and agree to discuss it in a few days' time.

- Don't feel it all has to be sorted in one all-purpose conversation.

Below, I suggest some of the possible things you can do. They won't all appeal to you and my list is certainly not exhaustive – it's there for you to add to it. Just because you're going to a sun spot doesn't mean you have to spend the whole time on the beach wistfully looking at small children with their parents making sandcastles and wishing you could do it all over again, or lying there reminding each other of the good old times when the children were small.

And there's nothing stopping you doing things independently. He may like to fish; you might like surfing or shopping. Decide in advance on two individual pursuits while you're away. Doing different things during the day will certainly give you something to talk about in the evening. That's one solution to the prospect of conversation drying up. Another might be to read the same book and then discuss it with each other. You could also try taking it in turns to choose where you're going to eat and 'take' each other there – a bit like playing at having a date! And you may be able to afford one really nice night out now there are just two of you and not four or five.

One of the patterns couples often adopt is keeping conversations bland so there are no disagreements. This can stifle our thinking and healthy debate. Agree with each other that it's all right to have different opinions, that there doesn't have to be a 'winner'. The key is to be genuinely open with and interested in each other. If you're not competing, the conversation becomes stimulating and enriching.

Have some sex! One area of life that often gets neglected when we have children is sensual pleasure and sex. One thing you can do when you're alone is spend some time enjoying each other's body. Many of us find we're too tired or stressed with our everyday lives to indulge in sex, which either stops or gets rushed without any real enjoyment. This holiday could be your opportunity to rekindle that part of your relationship. It's an area where talking isn't needed (so that solves one problem!). For most of us, when we're having good sex with our lover, we find that conversation flows if we want it to and, when it doesn't, that's just fine.

You started by saying that you'd already booked your holiday for this year and that you'd booked where you always do. Even choosing your holiday can become a habit if you aren't careful. Next year, you might want to think of something different, something you couldn't have done with young children or couldn't have afforded. (See Section 6, Question 4 on habits.)

A wealth of different types of holiday have sprung up for the over-fifties. There are activity holidays of every sort and numerous centres that offer such a variety that both of you will find something you want to do. You could go to a summer school and learn a new hobby or undertake some study. Or to a language school and learn a language you've always wanted to speak.

Then there are a number of charities that look for cyclists or walkers to do sponsored walks in exotic places. You'll meet new people and raise money. Lots of organisations now ask for volunteers to come and work for them for one or two weeks at a school in India, say, or at a conservation centre in Borneo, or taking a group of children or people with a disability on holiday. No special skills are required.

Going on an organised trip specially designed for the older (not old) person means the activities will meet your physical requirements. Those who want to climb the Himalayas can, while those who want to watch turtles on the beaches of the Galapagos Islands can opt for that. And remember: you don't have to take every holiday with your partner. Now you're freer, you can each do your own thing and then join each other for holidays together at other times. In Section 5, Question 7 I talk about taking longer breaks, which become more possible for many of us as we get older. There are a number of good sources of information in the Resource List.

Bon voyage!

Q8 I am going to be 50 in three years. I never had children, not because I was putting it off but I never met the right man. I have now and we'd love a family of our own. Do you think I've missed the boat? If not, what should I do?

This is a tricky question. I've always believed that we're never too old to do anything and that we shouldn't let age hold us back. If you want to go hang-gliding at 90, why not? But the whole issue of late motherhood certainly challenges many people's beliefs. Although doctors in the UK are generally against women of your age conceiving, in Europe, there are a number of doctors who feel the woman should choose, not the medics. We've all read about women who've had babies in their sixties and are thrilled.

You ask if you have missed the boat. That's something for you and your doctor to discover; and the sooner you find that out, the sooner you'll be able to start making some decisions. As to whether you should try to get pregnant at this age, only you and your partner can decide. Without any doubt, though, there's been a shift towards delaying parenthood. Less than thirty years ago, women were told they were older mothers when they had a baby beyond the age of 28 and they were treated differently as they were seen to be more at risk.

According to a detailed analysis of birth statistics for England and Wales (published in December 2005 by the Office for National Statistics) there are now more 30- to 34-year-olds having their first child than those in the 25- to 29-year-old bracket, while the number of children born to women in the 40 to 44 age range has increased by 50 per cent over the last decade. The number of children born to women over 45 went up from 488 in 1994 to 909 in 2004; of these, 133 were born to women over 48 but only 48 to mothers over 50.

There always have been older mothers but usually these were people who already had children and may have had a late child by accident. Rarely did a 40+ woman actively seek to conceive. However, the number of attempts to become pregnant through IVF in women aged over 50 and the number born to them increased 24-fold between 1992 and 2002. These figures look set to go on rising. The UK figures are mirrored by those in the US, Australia, Canada and Europe. So, although you'd be at the far end of the scale, you'd by no means be alone. This is important, as everyone needs support when they first have children. The likelihood is that your own mother, if she's still alive, will be elderly and not as able to help you as she might have been 20 years ago.

We also need to be straight about the facts. As we get older, we become less fertile. This starts around 30 and it usually takes older women longer to conceive. By the time you get to your mid- and late forties and early fifties, the chance of your conceiving naturally or using your own eggs is increasingly unlikely. If you agree to an egg donation, your child won't have your genes but would be carried by you and given birth to by you. But that child will have the genes of your partner. That may not seem fair but that is the way nature created us.

Although our bodies can't do the process naturally, it's not an overly complicated technical procedure to create a pregnancy in a menopausal or post-menopausal woman. HRT is used to stimulate the womb before a donor egg from a young woman is inserted. Those are the medical facts but it isn't, of course, the whole story.

Some people feel this type of intervention is not natural and therefore not acceptable. As a society, we can be hypocritical about it being unnatural for women to become older parents but fine for men. But men also age and become ill. If children need both parents, which I believe they do, then there seems to me no logic why it should be unacceptable for women to have their children late and all right for men. Sure, women may need medical intervention but, in the end, is that so different from any other intervention – a heart bypass, for instance, or a hip replacement?

Once you've conceived, then there's the pregnancy. There'll be some inevitable wear and tear on your body. An older mother can be more prone to high blood pressure, osteoporosis, diabetes brought on by the pregnancy, and late bleeding that leads to an early delivery and additional intervention at the birth. All these factors can be detrimental to both the baby's and mother's health.

It's also well known that older women run a higher risk of the child having Down's syndrome and other less common genetic disorders. However, as a woman of your age may be conceiving using a young donor's egg, some of that risk may be reduced. There are also excellent screening systems that can detect many abnormalities early on. So you can make informed choices and most babies, if they get to near enough full term, are fine, whatever the age of the mother.

There's a fierce debate going on about whether it's good for a child to have such an old (in our societal view) mother. There's no doubt that a 50-year-old father would scarcely merit a second glance. So why the sexism? As discussed elsewhere, many of us feel 18 on a good day, even if we're 50+ so we'd probably cope pretty well. And there are definite advantages in being a mature woman with clear values and principles when embarking on the parental journey.

You're more likely to have a good sense of self and what you want in life and, after all, you did make a positive, well thought-out decision to embark on this route. However, some aspects of mothering may come as a bit of a shock. Being with your baby 24/7 is rather different from having a job! Lack of sleep night after night can also be exhausting whatever your age and certainly when you're older. Money won't be flowing into the household like before if you choose either to live on one income or pay for childcare. Travelling, dinners out and trips to the theatre and cinema will be much reduced. On the other hand, you'll almost certainly be perfectly content to be at home with your precious prize. Unlike many younger mothers, you'll probably have done most of the things you've wanted to do and won't be restlessly waiting until you can get going on achieving your goals.

Results from a small study undertaken by the University of North Carolina, published on the internet in 2006, revealed that women who give birth in their fifties are just as healthy, both physically and psychologically, as those who start families much younger. There was nothing to suggest any difference in how well a mother copes with her children at any given age and, in some instances, older mothers manage better and with less stress. Some of the perceived negative thinking and anxieties are due to no more than people's prejudices.

But babies grow into children and young adults. They're around for at least eighteen years and some for a lot longer! If you have your child when you're 50, you'll be nearly 70 when he or she leaves school. We all know that teenagers are rarely the easiest people to be around. Staying up till 3 a.m. worrying where they are is highly stressful for the younger parent, let alone someone nearing 70, although there's no reason why you won't be up to the challenge.

You also need to be aware that most of the mothers with children your children's age will be much younger than you. If you feel comfortable with that so will they. You'll need a new peer group even if you already have a lot of good friends as you'll find your life will be out of sync with them for quite a while. Some will be looking forward to grandchildren and will therefore be in a very different place from you.

If you and your partner, having weighed up all the arguments, think you can make good parents, my feeling is there's no reason why you should hold back on your dream. Good luck.

Q9 **I am 59 with two children aged 18 and 19. I have been dating a lovely man for four months. My children have seen him once when he picked me up. He stays with me or me with him when the children are at their father's (we have been divorced for two years). I would like my children to meet my man properly and for him to stay over at times when they're there, too. I don't think it will be that long before we're ready to live together and even marry. How do I introduce the idea to my children?**

With the divorce rate worldwide rising all the time, many of us will be faced with this situation as well as meeting another person's children. Reconstituted or blended families are commonplace. Almost two-thirds of re-marriages include children from a previous relationship so patchwork families are a growing phenomenon.

The number of long-established relationships coming to an end has grown and given rise to a new trend. This is turn has affected the number of older children whose parents split up, so many youngsters in their teens and early twenties are affected. Men in their late thirties and mid-forties are now as likely to divorce as those under 30. Around a quarter of women in their early forties have now gone through a divorce (ONS Population Trends 125). Because people are generally living longer, a person in their fifties who is either divorced or in an unhappy relationship doesn't relish the thought of thirty years or so living on their own or in a difficult relationship. Sexual activity doesn't stop because you're 60 or 70!

But back to your question. My initial reaction is, 'Slow down!' You talk about all the steps in one breath. This is a sensitive area and can be very upsetting if it goes wrong so you need to think and plan carefully. That doesn't mean it will necessarily be easy and without any tensions but it does mean you and your new partner will have given it your best shot.

All of us, however open and non-judgemental we think we are, make judgements when we meet someone new. What we try to do is not to let these judgements colour our behaviour, but that can be tricky. Think of a time when you met someone at a friend's house and you took an instant dislike to them. You didn't actually know them but they nonetheless sparked a negative reaction. Sometimes, this initial reaction sticks for ever; sometimes, it changes but very slowly. It takes much longer to change someone from a negative feeling to thinking positively than the other way around. So remember, first impressions count.

I do think you're right in the way that you haven't tried to force your new man on to your children too quickly. From what you say, you've already spent a bit of time with this man and know that the relationship is feeling serious with long-term possibilities. For those of you who met someone last week, take a leaf out of our questioner's book. Get to know them first before you involve the children.

Much as when you and their father split up, it was not your children's choice and I expect you made it very clear to them that you weren't separating from them, just from each other. This new situation is the same, just the other way around. It's you who've met someone new and fallen for him. The children didn't choose either him or the timing. It's a bonus if they all really like each other and something you can certainly play a part in assisting but it's not their choice and it never was.

If asked, most children of divorced parents, whatever their age, will say that, in an ideal world, if their parents didn't fight, cheat on each other, drink too much and so on, they'd prefer them to stay together. The loss and longing we have for our parents to stay with each other come from the child part inside us. (See Section 4, Question 1.) It may be irrational, but it's still a valid feeling.

Children are likely to feel some jealousy and fear that their mum will be taken away from them. They may well have been hoping that you and their father would get together again. Introducing someone new causes distress to 'children' of any age. I recently heard of a 54-year-old man with four children of his own and a wife. When his widowed mother of 78 wanted to introduce him to a man she had started 'dating', he was so appalled he initially refused to see her, and still won't meet the man!

You say that they've seen your friend briefly in passing but not as yet spent any time with him. Nonetheless, they do know there's someone around. I'm sure they have lots of mixed emotions but they're bound to be curious. Have you discussed introductions with your new bloke? The focus of this meeting has to be for the children so that their interests come first. It's a good time to see how able he is to suspend his needs and anxieties and empathise with your children.

Neutral environments are the best. As your kids are a bit older, I'd suggest a trip to the cinema. Choose the type of film they like and then possibly go for a snack afterwards, which will give you the chance for a short chat about the film without having to fill a whole evening. At the end of the evening, go home with the children. Don't bring him home. In the back of your children's minds, that would look as if he were moving in, especially as you say he's stayed before and will inevitably demonstrate that he knows the house. (One word of warning: don't choose a Friday, when teenagers like to go out with their mates.)

Don't hurry the meetings. Let a few days pass before you all meet again. If he's going to be part of your life, then a few more weeks of seeing less of him than you'd like won't matter. Keep the meetings low-key and no post mortems with your children asking them what they think of him. Your intuition will tell you how it's going.

Help your bloke to be cool about it, too. There's nothing worse than the person who's trying too hard. Remind him (and educate him, if he hasn't had children of his own) that your kids aren't looking for a new pal for themselves. They don't expect him to have the same taste in music or want him to stay up clubbing three nights over a weekend or hear a joke from him that makes them squirm. Keep your relationship non-physical in front of them, especially at the beginning, and then very, very gradually become a little more tactile.

Your children are of an age when they may have already been exploring sexual relationships for themselves. It's a time for them to grow and begin to understand their own desires and wishes. They won't want to think of their parents as sexually active and the last thing either of them will want to hear about is your sex life. It's tempting, especially if you've got into the habit of talking to them about your feelings since you've been on your own, to imagine you can share your developing relationship with them. But, while I'm not suggesting that you pretend it isn't happening, please be discreet.

They may also feel slightly put out that your love life is almost running in parallel with theirs. Your children are very nearly grown-up so, if your chap's going to stay, give them plenty of warning. That way, if either of them feels at all uncomfortable, they can make arrangements to sleep over with a friend for the night. It helps at all times if they feel consulted. And make sure you don't have double standards: if you can have your long-term boyfriend to stay, so can they.

Make sure they always know they're really important to you, that you'll continue doing for them what you've always done. This really is essential. And, even if you do so, they may well be jealous of your new bloke and at times him of them. It's a difficult juggling act.

The important thing is to talk about your feelings, not to side with anyone, to keep an open mind and trust that it'll work. Although your children may feel as though their nose has been put a little out of joint, they'll have your wellbeing at heart and will want you to be happy. They're just about to embark on their own lives and knowing that you're happy and settled will be very liberating for them.

You haven't mentioned this but often in new relationships of this sort there will be his children, too. That adds another dimension that has to be taken into consideration. You need to follow all the same principles as he does when meeting your children.

The more considerate you are of the children's feelings, the more likely it is everything will work out fine. Despite any preconceptions you may have, step-parents can have a really positive effect on their step-children's lives. They offer new perspectives, new interests. However involved, they're also less emotionally embroiled so are often able to see both sides of a situation and have an objective and caring viewpoint. Many a step-parent has acted as a mediator in an adolescent row. A number of women have told me that their new partner has helped them understand their children's point of view and saved a real upset. So, while you might not have predicted your life would have gone this way, a lot of good things can flow from your new situation.

Q10 **I'm in my early sixties and was widowed a couple of years ago after 36 years of marriage. Now I've fallen in love again – and really deeply in love, just like a 15-year-old. I find myself anxiously sitting by the phone to speak to him or checking for his emails. I've lost my appetite and I feel sexier than I have for years, although I do worry a bit about having sex. My friends think I'm over the top because at our age we should be looking for companionship not romance and certainly not sex. Is that really the case? I've no one to ask. I'm beginning to feel I'm a bit odd because I'm so in love.**

However old you are, starting a new relationship makes you feel as though you're a teenager again. Feeling sexy and in love is not age-dependent; the same feelings occur at any age. What a bore your friends are! I'm tempted to say they're envious. There will be those who are in long-term relationships where sex may no longer be exciting. The reason they say companionship is the answer is because that's what they've settled for and they see themselves as right. Others may be single and wishing it was happening to them.

In no way am I wanting to put a damper on these delicious feelings but understanding that they have a chemical basis may help you to see that what you're doing is not out of the ordinary, just normal. When we're stimulated by someone whom we find attractive, a small cluster of nerves in an area called the hypo-thalamus transmits a chemical message to our pituitary gland at the base of our brain, which in turn sends its chemicals into the bloodstream. As these hormones move through our system, they reach the organs that respond sexually and these parts then send out more hormonal messages and our body becomes aroused. Our heartbeat increases, we feel a lightness in our heads and a corresponding response in our genitals and breasts.

This all happens quickly. If it's a one-minute fantasy, it'll be over almost before it's begun. But, if the feeling persists, that's when you'll start the process of falling in love. So let's get this straight: it's physiological and, while you have a brain that's able to be stimulated, you'll have these feelings. And you can experience this biochemically based high whatever your age. There's nothing weird about that.

With 60 being the new 40 and 80 the new 60, you've got lots more years of romantic and sexual feelings to enjoy. As a new relationship develops, the rose-tinted glasses come off and, if all goes well, your feelings will grow and mature. The physical side of the relationship will begin to calm down, which doesn't mean you'll never get turned on again but not all the time!

The feelings of no appetite are all a part of what you're going through. The chemical system tends to suppress the appetite as well which, for some of us, is a plus when we want to look our best. I often think of those meals to which I was taken out at the start of a relationship when a new boyfriend wanted to impress. I'd pick at the food, moving it around the plate not wanting to look rude.

Some of us experimented with sex, drugs and rock 'n' roll in the sixties, while others followed in our mothers' footsteps and – sexually inexperienced – married young. Monica Morris in her book *Falling in Love Again – The Mature Woman's Guide to Finding Romantic Fulfilment* says that, once widowed, her expectations had been of a celibate life. She was surprised when she found herself doing something that she had never expected: she started dating again.

Normally, we learn a skill and then practise it. But marriage puts paid to dating so no wonder people back on the singles market feel a little awkward. She says that she, like many of us, had been led to believe that there are so many more women looking for men to date than there are men that it was unlikely she'd ever meet anyone again. Prophecy then becomes the reality. Monica Morris's book sorts out the myths and gives many useful tips for finding love as a mature person and dealing with it maturely, too.

One area where I think a little caution may be needed (and your friends' concern valid) would be if your romance were only to be conducted on the internet and not in person. I'm sure you can fall in love with someone you haven't met but, if they live thousands of miles away, packing up your whole life to go and live in, say, Australia when you haven't met them seems a little rash. In that instance, it would be wise to go and visit for a holiday or, even better, get them to come and visit you.

All right, so we're agreed that you're not doing anything out of the ordinary for a 60-year-old in 2008. If you talk to doctors, they'll tell you that, twenty years ago, most women felt that, by the time they reached 60, sex was over for them and most men weren't far behind. But the baby boomers were there at the start of the sexual revolution and they haven't stopped yet.

There are two reasons this has happened. First, we are living longer – and healthier too. Second, during the last decade, there have been amazing strides in helping people rediscover their sex lives. Since you mention that you're a bit worried about having sex as you're not sure whether everything is working just as it should, a good person to consult is your GP. Doctors are there both to offer you medicine if needed and also to listen. Well Women clinics are also very good sources of information and support.

There's a lot, however, that you can do for yourself. Regular exercise at the gym, swimming or going for long walks, losing a few pounds in weight (we often put on a bit at the start of the menopause), watching your diet and eating and drinking a bit less can all contribute to an enhanced feeling of greater well-being. Just a couple of weeks of taking yourself in hand can make your body look fitter and sexier while making you feel so much better about yourself. And, if you're feeling good, you'll worry less about the bits that don't work quite as efficiently as they once did.

For many of us, once the menopause approaches, there's some reduction in vaginal secretions and some of us can become very dry. You may well benefit from using any of a large number of vaginal preparations that are on sale at the chemist or by mail order. This is one area that we often don't talk about and many women become quite anxious, as sexual intercourse can make you sore. As a result, it's easy to assume that we're no longer sexually responsive. That's not true although, if you do experience some soreness, it's much less likely you'll have an orgasm. If the over-the-counter products don't help alleviate the problem, talk to your GP about vaginal hormone creams or pessaries, which usually work extremely well.

The menopause brings hot flushes for many of us and some women worry about having one during sex. They're a normal part of a woman's ageing process and I don't think a bit of sweating has ever put anyone off. If you have other anxieties – and less-than-good bladder control, tiredness or backache so that many sexual positions are uncomfortable – talk to your GP, the practice nurse or a sex therapist.

Just a word before you throw all caution to the wind: remember about sexually transmitted diseases. Sexual infections in the over-fifties has trebled in the past five years including chlamydia, herpes and HIV. HIV education was not given to us when we were young as it wasn't an issue. Although we were all around for the campaigns of the eighties and early nineties, many of us felt it wasn't relevant to us because of our marital status and so may not have taken on board how to have safer sex. It's very unlikely that you'll be having sex with a 60-year-old virgin so you do need to practise safer sex. The Family Planning Association, NHS Direct and other health organisations will have all the information you need.

I've raised a few of the possible difficulties that might occur so you're aware of them but don't let any of this put you off. Where the heart is willing, even if the body creaks a bit, you'll definitely find a way to find sexual fulfilment. And don't listen to your friends. Just get out there and enjoy. Who knows? You may well be able to give them some advice and help them to think beyond companionship.

Section Four

You're Never Too Old to...
Juggle Life

Throughout our lives, we will at times take stock of where we are and where we're going to. Coming up to 50 and then 60 are definitely milestones for reflection and assessment. We're assailed by all sorts of questions.

We ask ourselves, 'What have I done with my life so far?' and 'What am I doing with my life now?' and 'How many different roles do I play? I'm worker, partner, mother, carer, volunteer.

Are these the roles I want to go on playing?' And finally, 'How will these roles change over the next few years and how am I going to shape my future?'

Many of us spent a lot of our thirties and forties running to keep up. Ten or twenty years on, one of the great pluses is that those who took a career break are back in the workplace, the equal of our male colleagues. The downside is that too often we're still the ones keeping an eye on the children, managing the house and caring for elderly relatives. The recurrent dilemma seems to be how do we juggle the conflicting demands of our lives without being overwhelmed by everyone else's demands. The following heartfelt question is typical:

Q1 My mother is coming up to 85. She never expected to reach this age. Most of her parents' generation died younger. I realise it's likely that I will get to my eighties and quite probably my nineties. If I do, my children will be in their sixties. My mother and I have never managed to change our relationship: she still tells me off and makes me feel about five years old! I don't want it to be like this when I'm 90 and my children are 60. How can I do it differently?

This is the $64 million question as far as I'm concerned! If we can crack this one, we'll really have changed family relationships. Most people's learning about relationships, communication and values takes place within the context of the family. In the late 1940s and 1950s, when the baby boomers were born, people's roles and the way they were expected to behave were very clearly defined. There was a definite demarcation line between the generations. A young person would never call their next-door neighbour by their first name: it would always be Mr or Mrs and the surname. Aunts and uncles would never be called by their first name alone and close family friends were given honorary titles of 'aunt' or 'uncle' to show a special position and a little respect.

Families were very hierarchical, with grandparents at the head. Even within peer generations, there was a hierarchy with older siblings often left to look after younger ones and therefore expecting a similar respect. Just being a member of one of those groups gave you certain roles and expectations.

Today's world is very different. The youth culture starting with the baby boomers has promoted an idea that younger people are better, more full of energy, more technologically adept and more business-minded: something that has certainly been taken on board by our children's generation. Shifts have been seen within families and generations. For example, our parents, teachers and carers generally assumed they 'knew best' whereas we tend to relate to our children in a more consensual way, accepting that the younger person has valid ideas. But I don't think we have, by any means, totally dropped the behaviour of our parents.

Things are certainly different. Many young people do not settle down into long-term relationships or raise a family till later in life. They have more years without other responsibilities and many of them live at home well into their twenties. Figures from the Office for National Statistics (ONS Social Trends 33) show that on average women are not getting married until they're 29 as compared to 23 in the 1960s. There is also a similar increase in age for men.

Average Age at Marriage	Average Age of Mother at Childbirth	
	1st child	All births
1961 – Men 25.6 Women 23.1		
1971 – Men 24.6 Women 22.6	1971 – 23.7	26.6
1981 – Men 25.4 Women 23.1	1981 – 24.8	27.0
1991 – Men 27.5 Women 25.5	1991 – 25.6	27.7
2000 – Men 30.5 Women 28.2	2001 – 26.6	28.6
2005 – Men 31.0 Women 29.0	2005 – 27.3	29.0

Alongside this, people of our generation are also wanting to live differently. Many of us are unprepared to fall into the stereotype of an older person and do not plan to live life in a conventional way. This will include working past retirement age as well as having time to travel and pursue other interests. So our external world is changing, but are we truly changing within ourselves?

I think to understand what is going on, it would be useful to look at a psychological theory created by Eric Berne, called Transactional Analysis. I will explain the relevant areas in answering your question. It suggests that within each one of us we have a parent part, an adult part and a child part whether we are 2 or 102. These are known as ego states. Each ego state has specific behaviours that are associated with it while each one of us has elements of our personality which surface and affect our behaviour according to different circumstances.

Parent	Behaviours, thoughts and feelings learnt from parents/parental figures
Adult	Behaviours, thoughts and feelings which are direct responses to the here and now
Child	Behaviours, thoughts and feelings replayed from childhood

The parent is our internal voice of the authority, learning and attitudes we absorbed when we were young. Like it or not, we're inevitably conditioned by our parents, teachers, older people, next-door neighbours, aunts and uncles and those who pass on their beliefs and values. Our inner parent is formed by all the external events and influences on us as we grew up. The parent has two parts that can be subdivided into the positive part which embraces caring and nurturing and the negative which involves controlling, structuring and criticising.

The adult is our ability to think and determine action for ourselves, based on received data. The adult is straightforward and non-emotional. It draws on the resources of both the other ego states to help us make informed decisions.

The child is our internal reaction to and feelings about external events. This is the seeing, hearing, feeling and emotional body of data within each of us. When anger or despair dominates reason, the child is in control. There are several parts to it: the adapted part that is cooperative and wants to please; the rebellious, resistant part that is not so positive; the free, spontaneous part that can have fun and enjoy and be creative; and the immature part that can't see reason.

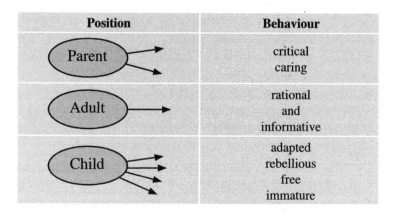

Position	Behaviour
Parent	critical caring
Adult	rational and informative
Child	adapted rebellious free immature

In summary:

- The parent is our 'taught' concept of life.

- The adult is our 'thought' concept of life.

- The child is our 'felt' concept of life.

We communicate from one of our ego states whether parent, adult or child. Our feelings at the time determine which one we use, and at any time something can trigger a shift both from one to another and from one part to another. When we respond, we're also doing this from one of the three states.

When communicating, one person can be communicating from their parent part while another can be communicating from their child part. This can lead to miscommunication. We each tend to operate from a preferred state, and not always the most appropriate one – especially when stressed. Different environments can also change which part we use.

When our children were young it was appropriate for us in the main to be in the parent position, caring for them, teaching them and telling them off when it was warranted. We were their teachers and their role models. Similarly, in our relationships with other adults, our intention on a daily basis is to behave in an adult manner and to be rational and logical. However, other states can be triggered unconsciously by something that is said or by the particular environment.

It sounds like you only need to *think* about your mother, let alone *see* her, and you become your five year old person and the mother becomes the critical parent. The communication will therefore be of a child and their parent. The response is automatic and it probably feels as though there's no choice about how to behave. To change this pattern of behaviour with your own children, it's essential to relate to them from the adult – rather than the parent – position, which will automatically elevate your children and bring them into the adult state as well.

I'm not saying that there's never an appropriate time to be critical and/or caring. There are times when it's absolutely appropriate to respond in one of these ways but sometimes, through habit, people fall into this position when it's totally inappropriate. Children respond to parents so, if you behave like a parent, they'll respond either as an 'adapted' child who wants to please and make amends with the parent or authority figure, or as the rebellious child who tells you to get lost.

The challenge for us is to learn to be adult with our children (when they're adults) even when we're tempted to tell them how they should behave or muscle in when it should be their partner looking after them, not their mother. If we can do that, things will get better. It's going to take some practice so my advice is to start now, in which case you'll have got there before your children are 50+ and you're 85!

Q2 **My husband is getting very fed up with me as I feel I have to spend a lot of my free time with my elderly father who's lonely and not that well. I can see this is having an adverse effect on my marriage and neither is it great for my kids. I just don't know how to juggle things.**

Welcome to the sandwich generation! I think what you're talking about is feeling like the filling in the middle. This is yet another new phenomenon that's happening to many of us. For a start, we married later and had children later than our parents. Alongside this, life expectancy has changed. Between 1981 and 2002, life expectancy at age 50 increased by 4.5 years for men and 13 years for women. By 2002, women who were aged 65 could expect to live to 84, and men to 81.

If you had your children when you were in your thirties or even early forties, you will have school-aged children at the same time as elderly parents who may need support, care and attention. You'll be sandwiched between these two demands. Even if your children are older, many of them are struggling financially. The price of housing in the UK is so high that they often stay at home until well into their twenties or they may leave home then return because they've run up debts, can't afford the rent or can't get into the job market.

They're the new 'boomerang' generation who are finding it difficult to manage economically on their own. Parents find themselves having to subsidise accommodation, and graduates who have a low income feel frustrated and inadequate that they're unable to become independent. Furthermore, working practices have also changed as have the expectations of young men and women both at home and at work. Things were very different in the 1950s when 19.5 per cent of women were working. By 1965, 51 per cent of women were working although mostly part time, but by 2003, that figure had risen to 73 per cent (www.statistics.gov.uk).

Although the sixties brought a radical shift in thinking and in the relationships between men and women due to the women's liberation movement, the fact is that a lot of our parents and in-laws still believe that their 'girl' children should be the homemaker and that, if they work, it will probably be for pin money and their work is unimportant. Their expectations are that we will be there to look after them in their old age. These were the belief systems our parents were brought up on and brought us up on. They were part of their and our conditioning.

The difference was that we were part of the sixties movement. And so we're torn. Part of us thinks we should be running to look after our parents and part of us thinks we shouldn't have to. We have to juggle, not knowing how to meet what we believe are our responsibilities – such as how to take a parent to a hospital appointment, go to a school play or sports day while also meeting our business commitments. It's tricky but it needs to be tackled so you can feel good about yourself and maintain healthy relationships. (Question 1 of this section, parent, adult, child, explains the psychology of the situation.)

You say 'you feel that you have to', not that your father is telling you to spend all your time with him so it's you who has to learn not to feel that way and not to feel guilty. (Also see Question 4, which discusses these issues.) Your father is lonely. Is it up to you to fill that space for him? He is also unwell. Is it your role to be the nurse? What are our responsibilities towards our elderly parents who have cared and nurtured us when we were young? Was the deal we bought into that we would look after them? Is that the deal you see for your own children? That you gave to them and now they give to you? If not, why should it be like that for you?

When you married and moved away from home, your relationship with your parents changed and your partner rightly became the primary relationship. If children followed, caring for them until they were old enough to do it for themselves was the priority. I don't understand why this has to change because our parents become less independent. I am not advocating that you should ignore your father. What I think you need to do is get it in balance with your life.

Here's a useful question to ask yourself: if this was a close friend of yours who was having to juggle an elderly parent, husband, children and job, what would you be advising them? What other help should they be enlisting? It's important at times like this for you to stay true to your beliefs and values without doing something because you feel you ought to. By looking at the problem as though it was someone else's, we invariably come up with an answer untainted by guilt.

So let's think practically for a moment. What does your father need? He needs company and probably some help in the house. Does this all have to be done by you? There are organisations like Help the Aged that are there to support you and your father. Also your GP and social services will be able to offer some assistance. (See the Resource List.) You don't mention if you have siblings. In families, care of this sort very often falls to one person. This is probably a role you have always taken. That doesn't mean you have to go on doing so. Share the visiting with your siblings; they can help, too. There are also lots of agencies that arrange volunteer visitors who will spend time with your father. They usually match people up so they have the same interests. Your father, in spite of loving your visits, might welcome other stimulating conversation.

Discuss the problem with all concerned and see if you can find a solution that suits you all. Ask your husband what it is that he really minds. Is it that you're out all the time? Or is that, when you're together, you both complain about how tired you are with all you have to do and you constantly talk about your father? See if you can compartmentalise it (something men do better than women) and not bring your father home, so to speak, unless it's a crisis.

Without wanting to sound harsh, this is your choice. You can see what's happening and, as I'm sure you know, marriage takes work and time. The likelihood is that your marriage will still be there when your father has passed on so try to take the long view.

Of course, we mustn't forget our children's needs. The deal from their point of view is that they should come first. On the other hand, as children grow up, they need to learn to think about and care about other people apart from themselves. They could help you with their grandfather by visiting him occasionally or chatting to him on the phone. It's a good opportunity to learn while young to respect old people. They wouldn't be here if it weren't for their grandparents!

For those of you reading this who have not yet got to this potential predicament because your parents are well and fit, take note and start planning. Unless they die youngish, you're likely to be faced with parents who deteriorate either physically or mentally or, perhaps, both. Plan ahead, check out the resources, talk to your parents and think through what might have to be done so that everybody's needs are taken into account.

Q3 **Due to the ageing of my mother (my father died many years ago), my siblings and I have had to make decisions together about her care and about her home. I find myself having to make decisions with people who have totally different values from mine. What are the communication tricks I can use to keep conflict at a minimum? I find myself behaving as we did when we were children. How do we learn to be adult together? We have had years to do it but are nowhere near how I'd like us to be.**

This must feel quite tough. At the moment, it must be hard enough having to deal with ageing parents without having to cope with siblings who seem to be making things so much more difficult. I expect each of you is feeling the same. I discuss family relationships in Question 1 of this section, so do familiarise yourself with the concept there from Transactional Analysis of 'parent, adult and child'. In order to manage this, you need to talk and think from your adult self and not your child self. From what you say, you have all reverted to children.

In families there is a hierarchy in the pecking order of siblings. The natural 'leaders' are often the eldest and the youngest is usually seen as the baby, as well as the one who was closest to the mother (which doesn't mean had the best relationship) and so on. In some families, there will be such a large age range that the baby arrived just before the eldest left so their relationship has never been close and the youngest is still thought of as little older than a toddler. Coupled with the old family history will be all your thoughts – about cost of care, money and inheritance – none of which is easy and all subjects that have probably never been discussed. You also all have to come to terms with the power shifts now that your mother is less well. One or more of you may have taken Power of Attorney or need to and that changes the balance of power in the family.

Looking at the list of possible issues, which is by no means comprehensive, it's not surprising everyone has fallen back into their old patterns of behaviour: at least your behavioural patterns feel familiar! They're the ones you learnt as children around your parents, your default positions, the ones you go into when stressed or upset. They're also the ones you all know don't work.

Every one of us has had experience of having to make decisions with people with whom we don't see eye-to-eye and yet nego-tiate some sort of agreement. But that is usually at work and so we just don't have the same emotional connection.

It sounds to me as if everyone has his or her own idea with the result that winning becomes more important than the outcome. So sibling A might say something, and then sibling B and C will put forward a counter argument. If they agree with each other, sibling A feels picked on and becomes even more defensive. Usually, when we're trying to prove a point, we say, 'Yes, but . . .' when what we really mean is, 'NO, I don't agree!' thereby negating everything before the 'but'.

A very useful technique in negotiation is to say, 'Yes, and . . .' which tells the other person you've listened and you're simply adding another suggestion and defusing a possible argument.

Listening to what people say is really important, although just because you've listened doesn't mean you necessarily agree. It does, however, signal respect, which is crucial. Answer questions in a non-emotional manner with no overtones or undertones and other people will hear you as genuine. Be careful, though, with your non-verbal gestures. If you throw your eyes up to heaven when one of them speaks, you'll undermine all your good work.

A useful tip: if you're going to get anywhere and, before you start the detail of the discussion, you need to agree to agree! You have to trust that they want this to be sorted, too.

You all have different perspectives and are arguing because you have each become wedded to your own point of view which you know is right! In this position, we tend to set up polarisation. Yours and your siblings' goal has to be finding a 'win/win' solution where everyone feels the solution is possible. This means you have to accept that the outcome may be different from the one you initially envisaged or hoped for.

To encourage the kind of flexibility and openness needed for you to achieve a solution that is truly 'win/win', a good starting point is exchanging thoughts on the aims you all share: to achieve good care for your mother; and to remain friends, whatever the eventual outcome.

If your agreed aim is to find areas of common ground, you'll quite quickly discover what you like about each other which will help create a level of trust between you. As soon as you can accept and believe there could be common ground, a solution becomes possible. If not, you'll continue to argue just to prove the point that this is impossible.

Once you've agreed the aims, the next question has to be: 'What are the possible solutions?' A non-emotional and creative way to do this is to brainstorm all the possible solutions. It may sound more like a business meeting than a family get-together but that might be just what you need to keep the tensions at bay.

The rule is that no one is allowed to criticise anyone else's idea. At this point, anything goes. If you come up with some silly solutions – just for the fun of it – it'll make everyone laugh and a bit of humour is certainly needed. Now go through each idea in turn looking at how this could be a solution. You may find you need to do some research before a final solution can be made. Then agree who will do it and when you will come back to discuss your findings.

The following 12-point plan will really help you to get a good solution:

1. Offer each other mutual respect.

2. Put as much energy into understanding the others as you do into trying to be understood.

3. Actively seek and agree common ground.

4. Make concessions but not at the expense of feeling like the victim. (Victims usually moan and retaliate at a later stage.)

5. Be as open as possible and never defensive.

6. Explain why you think something. Don't expect other people to simply understand. Be clear and repeat things, if necessary.

7. Talk for yourself, not for your mother – there will be as many versions of your mother's views as siblings!

8. Avoid negativity and showing your negative feelings deliberately. Say what you mean – and avoid negative body language.

9. Use other people's language when talking to them and establish an early rapport. (See Section 5, Question 1.)

10. Give time to the discussion: never start when you've only got 20 minutes. Make sure everyone is clear about any decisions made. If you're in too much of a hurry, you could find that what you thought was agreed wasn't and you'll have to go back over old ground.

11. Instead of asking: 'How much will the care cost?' say: 'Can I ask a question?' Instead of just making a proposal, begin: 'If I could make a suggestion . . .' This approach draws the attention of the listener to what's coming and gently encourages a response. It also slows down negotiations and helps reduce the element of cut-and-thrust.

12. Don't make bitchy comments like 'I'd have expected you to say that,' and value-loaded expressions like 'It's not fair' or 'You're just being mean' will only irritate the very people you're trying to get to agree your point of view.

Sometimes, in these sorts of situation, it helps to have another family member who can help 'chair' the conversation. At other times, it can be a real advantage to have a mediator present. There are family mediators who can help you with this. Just because you have different values (or so it feels right now) doesn't mean that you want to fall out and have nothing more to do with those nearest (though not always dearest!) to you. If there's a possibility this might happen, get some help so you can all emerge with your friendship intact and with good decisions made.

If your mother is ill for a while, it is essential you learn how to do this now. Once you've re-learnt how to talk to each other, you'll all be fine. If you go on arguing, you will be in for a tough time: that is the reality. Remember also that the last thing your mother wants is to find her adult children at each other's throats. She needs you to be there for her rather than putting your energy into fighting.

Q4 I'm 55 years old and I've watched my mother with Alzheimer's deteriorate in front of my eyes. It has been extremely hard for me and my siblings. How do I make sure my children don't have to go through this with me or their father?

I'm so sorry. It is a horrible disease and one sadly that more and more of us will encounter. I fully understand you not wanting your children to have to face this. If we could decide our own fate, I expect most of us would like to live to our mid-eighties, be fit, healthy and with good energy and then die peacefully in our sleep. However, as we know, our future health is not something any of us can predict. What we can do, though, is arrange things to ease the burden on our children as we get older.

The following figures come from the Alzheimer's Society UK. They are a very useful resource for anyone who wants further information. Dementia currently affects over 750,000 people in the UK. Approximately 18,000 people with dementia are under the age of 65. Dementia affects 1 person in 20 over the age of 65 and 1 person in 5 over the age of 80. The number of people with dementia is steadily increasing. Alzheimer's disease is the most common form of dementia, making up 55 per cent of all cases. There are nearly 18 million people with dementia in the world.

I believe we, the baby boomer generation, have the opportunity to make some decisions about our old age and how we want to manage it. I personally don't subscribe to the view that our children have an obligation to look after us. I think the deal is that we look after them until they're of an age to look after themselves. (Some of us aren't very good at remembering that, but that's a different problem!)

You raise a very real dilemma for us all. How you cope will vary according to your life experience, the nature of your relationships and, of course, any first-hand knowledge of a degenerative disease that leads to dementia.

Many people's parents and particularly grandparents believed that it was the duty of the children to look after their parents. I remember an elderly man I knew when I was young who used to say a parent can look after seven children but seven children can't look after one parent! Even so, he believed that it was their duty to look after him. Unless you've personally been faced with a very elderly or dependent parent, I don't think this question will yet have crossed your mind but addressing potential problems while you're still fit and healthy could avoid much anxiety later.

Many of our generation have taken on the role of caring for elderly loved ones, feeling they have no choice and being both angry and sad about it rather than facing what this truly means in terms of their own lives. There is no right or wrong way in any of this. Each individual has to make their own decision. Whatever that may be, the important thing is that we think about it in advance.

I understand that you don't want your children to feel obligated to look after you. Having been in that situation yourself, you know that it can take over your life. Health and social services are stretched to the limit with an unprecedented demand and no further resources. This is likely to get worse unless more money is earmarked for them. Families are therefore called upon to manage the care more and more. Most of us are working and our children will be so they won't have the time to look after us (even if we and they want it).

I recently coached a man in his late fifties who works in what he describes as a 'young people's business'. He has a 92-year-old mother who has been very healthy but who was recently diagnosed with vascular dementia (a degenerative brain disorder). He's concerned about his position at work. As he's an only child, it has to be him. He wishes now that he and his mother had thought this through earlier.

It is, as many of us know, often a task that falls to women. Have we really fought long and hard for women's rights to find our daughters ending up being carers? For those who have done it, you know that it's often a thankless task as the parent loses their inhibitions and at times becomes aggressive and difficult. It's a fantasy that all old people, however difficult they have been in their lives, will turn into delightful geriatrics. We go on being exactly how we were but a more exaggerated version of it.

I've recently been discussing the question of old age with groups of women. One reported that her 78-year-old mother was living out of the UK as she felt it would be better for her health. She's not wealthy and lives frugally. She also felt she could be more independent and allow her children (to whom she is very close) to have their own lives. She's aware that there could come a time when she'll need looking after. So she's found a place for herself in sheltered accommodation where they have a care home attached for when you're no longer able to cope on your own.

All this has been done while she's hale and hearty. No one, there-fore, was going through the angst of managing an unwell mother, feeling guilty they didn't have time for her, or feeling resentful. She didn't do this on her own but as a result of a meeting she convened with all her children. As a result, her 50-year-old daughter felt valued and considered and under no obligation to do the caring for her parent. It was quite obvious from the way she spoke that she would be involved with her mother until the end, offering good-quality companionship and time. The perfect role model for us all!

In my experience, when children have to do the caring or manage the practicalities, the quality relationship goes out of the window. The son or daughter feels obligated to look after the parent. So much time is spent dealing with the practicalities and chores that there is precious little left over for any enjoyment. Unless we lay down agreed plans and actively put them in place in advance, there's no chance of it being different.

So when to do this? And when should we start preparing for old age? Many people I talk to have a fantasy that they'd like to live near their friends, possibly in the same block of flats or village, where they could look after each other and share daily help, have company nearby but also their own space. Sounds like a great idea to me but, if you really want to do it, you have to start well before you're too old to set in place your plans. If you wait until you're getting forgetful or your children are beginning to worry about you, you'll have missed the boat.

The best time to grasp the nettle? Maybe when you retire or perhaps even before. I personally think it is never too early to start this dialogue with your family and friends. Once it becomes part of the family consciousness, it will be far easier to implement and avoid so much potential heartache. (See the General Resource List for helpful organisations.)

Q5 **I'll be 50 this year. My life has not turned out as expected. I'm a single woman, I've had a couple of long-term relationships but no children and with no elderly parents to look after. I do have a couple of adolescent nieces and nephews and a handful of godchildren. I have some good friends but I'm worried about getting old, being on my own and feeling lonely. To be honest, I find myself getting a bit bored now. What can I do?**

I think most people, whatever their circumstances, would say, 'My life hasn't turned out as I expected,' maybe better or worse, but not like the daydream they had when they were growing up. I can see from what you say that there are experiences that are usually included in the fantasy that haven't happened to you. Most of us were brought up to believe we'd have a husband, 2.4 children, possibly work part time and, later, help in looking after our grandchildren.

When we reach any age with a new number at the front, we all do a life review. Fifty is a big one; it's the age we were brought up to regard as the last decade before winding down. It also marks for the majority of women the end of their child-bearing years. For some women, this is a positive turn of events but for others it will be one of life's losses and not just limited to those who've never had children. Either way, by this age we've done what we've done and we need now to focus on our present and future.

I'm going to answer your question in two parts as you pose two different questions. Let's start with loneliness. I found myself wondering whether it's future loneliness that frightens you or whether you're already feeling a bit lonely. You may have found yourself with a friendship group who are now mainly in relationships and with children to preoccupy them. You feel a bit bored and can't imagine how your life will entertain you in the future. You may feel you have got as far as you want at work and find you're not driven by further ambition. This might make you assume that this is how it will be when you're older. But nothing stays the same (one lesson we all learn as we get older) and you play a central role in your destiny.

Interestingly, a study undertaken by T. Koropeckyji-Cox Department of Population and Family Health Studies, Johns Hopkins University, USA in 1998 of 50- to 84-year-olds to look at 'whether childlessness is significantly related to loneliness or depression among older adults both alone and in conjunction to marital status' found that having no children was an explanation for loneliness in only a very small percentage of women. Those with higher levels of loneliness were divorced women and men and widowed men and women.

It was also found that 'The subjective wellbeing of never married childless men and women is indistinguishable from that of their married peers.' It's a societal myth that, if you don't have children, you'll be lonely when you get older, perhaps perpetuated by those who are struggling with theirs. If however, we buy into that belief (see Section 1, Question 1 for negative beliefs), we're more likely to walk straight into it and find ourselves lonely.

Loneliness is not the same as being alone. Loneliness is an emotional state where we feel overwhelmingly isolated and empty. It's more than just a longing for company or someone to do something with. Our self-esteem is usually pretty low and we feel sure there's something wrong with us. We often feel socially unskilled and inadequate. We're less assertive, convinced we've become invisible. We're reluctant to do anything new or make any changes.

Every one of us will at some point in our lives experience loneliness. Consider loneliness as a continuum of feelings, as defined by Sean Seepersad on his website www.webofloneliness.com. At one extreme is the person who rarely feels lonely but, when he or she does, Seepersad calls it 'state loneliness' – in other words, how you feel at that moment. This loneliness is generated more by the environment, by temporary circumstances, than by the person and usually doesn't last long. At the other extreme is the person experiencing loneliness all the time, as an inescapable part of their existence, which Seepersad defines as 'trait loneliness'. This is the type of loneliness that follows you everywhere. The loneliness is generated from within the person although particular circumstances might aggravate it. Because it's a feeling we all have at times, thousands of songs and poems have been written about it. The problem comes when the feeling goes on too long and we move from loneliness to depression. When depressed, it's hard to activate ourselves to do anything about it.

I think what you're concerned about is the feeling of being alone and sad about it, longing for something else. But it's a myth that being in a relationship stops you from feeling lonely. I talk to a lot of women who are desperately lonely but who are in what looks to the outside world like the perfect relationship. And yet they feel totally disconnected to everyone around them, craving what you have: time to be who you want to be and to make the choices you want to make.

I think a further influence for many of us is the pictures we see of lonely old people sitting passively either in their own homes with no one to talk to and no one to share life with or in an old people's home. I'm not going to talk about how we as a society treat the really old but suffice it to say that the images portrayed have a negative and depressing influence.

I think what you're saying is, 'I need to do something now with my life, change how it is and involve myself in different things so that I will have created a network of friends, family and activities that I can enjoy as I get older' – well, that sounds brilliant to me! You're in an excellent position, there's no one dependent on you and you're asking and thinking this now when you're young and healthy with time to plan. The world really is your oyster.

Section 1 has lots of ideas on how to plan your future but I think what you're probably looking for is some ideas of things you could do while you're contemplating your future direction. Here are ten ideas, not all of which will appeal!

1. Hone your dating skills. Read Section 3, Question 2 for some ideas of how to find an occasional or long-term lover as well as making some good friends along the way. Increasing your social circle takes you along avenues you have yet to explore.

2. Revamp your wardrobe and change your make-up. What you wear on the outside reflects who you are on the inside. If you want to bring something new into your life and to be treated differently, give out a different signal. (See Section 2, Question 2.)

3. Do something that inspires you. If you've always wanted to paint, go to art classes, or learn the language you've

always wanted to speak or join a rambling group or a local orchestra. Make sure that whatever you do takes you out of the house. It's so easy to get stuck in front of the internet and find a whole evening has gone.

4. Do some voluntary work and meet a whole new social circle and people who are living life very differently. You don't need any particular qualifications, just a bit of time to give to others. If you're missing elderly parents, 'adopt' some. There are lots of volunteer befriending organisations that match the older person with the visitor. The older person doesn't really want to be visited by a 15-year-old, lovely as they may be. They want someone with a bit more gravitas, a lot more life experience and some good conversation.

5. Take some time out and go on a retreat – there are lots advertised on the internet – and learn to meditate. This is a really good way to enjoy your own company and a skill you can fall back on in those bleak moments. Choose somewhere in a beautiful setting so you get an opportunity to enjoy the environment. Getting out into green open spaces, whether it's a park or the countryside, is a fantastic way to nourish the soul.

6. Do some exercise, either at the gym or local leisure centre. Go at the times of day when other single people may be there so you meet people who are in a similar position. Take up tennis or badminton.

7. Go to some of the 'life' shows that are held each year for the 50+, 'Fab at 50' (twice a year in Yorkshire and Bournemouth), for example, or 'One Life' (in London), which have a vast array of activities for baby boomers to enjoy. Look them up on the internet.

8. Keep up your with your extended family and close friends even if it seems they've less time available at the moment. Spend some quality time with your nieces, nephews and godchildren. There are probably one or two with whom you'd really connect. They'll be delighted to interact with a cool adult who isn't their parent, who's interested in them and who's willing to discuss without any emotional strings the things that matter to them.

9. Arrange a sabbatical from work (or unpaid leave) for at least six months, rent out your home and see the world. (See Section 5, Question 7.) But remember to keep in touch a little while you're away; by email is easiest.

10. Do something that you've never dared do before – step out of your comfort zone and try something that makes you feel proud to be 50.

Q6 **I'm in my mid-fifties and have always been very wrapped up in my children and my job. The kids have now all left home and I realise I've neglected a lot of my friends. I'm sad about this. But those who are still around I don't seem to have much in common with any more. How do you reconnect with old friends and make new ones at this stage of life?**

What is it about getting to our fifties and this belief that we instantly lose all the skills we ever had? So many people write saying 'at my age'. We really are our own worst enemy! We define ourselves as different and then wonder why others do the same.

I remember watching a mother with her over-boisterous son who could at times behave badly. She would arrive to visit friends and apologise in advance for all the things he might do. Later in the afternoon, when a child cried or a toy got broken, everyone assumed her son was the culprit. She, in turn, became despondent about the fact that he was always blamed. A wise member of the group took her aside and said, 'If you always tell us that he's badly behaved, we'll look out for it. You have the potential to be his best ambassador and yet you're giving him a bad press.' From that day, the mother started to praise his attributes and, not surprisingly, no one noticed his misdemeanours. You're guilty of the same self-fulfilling prophecy.

OK, speech over! Now let's get into discussing friendship. Many women tend to drop their loyal friends when they find a new compelling interest: not a charming trait. I'm sure you remember when your closest friend met a new partner and seemed to forget about you unless the partner was busy. You're 100 per cent right: we do all need friends. They enrich our lives and help us to feel part of the bigger world.

You want to make friends, or renew old friendships, and from what you say this time you plan to keep them. You're not alone. Even as early as the mid-1930s, Dale Carnegie wrote his highly acclaimed book *How to Win Friends and Influence People*. One of his main premises is that being genuinely interested in others and showing that you appreciate them is a sure-fire way of making them interested in you. This is a fundamental foundation of friendship.

But you must ask yourself what it is that you want friends for.

EXERCISE: WHY DO YOU WANT FRIENDS?

1.	Are you lonely and bored?	Yes/No
2.	Do you finding yourself wondering how old friends are doing?	Yes/No

3.	Have you got an ideal activity you want to do with a friend?	Yes/No
4.	Are you feeling isolated and scared that there's no one around?	Yes/No
5.	Do you want to share life experiences with someone?	Yes/No
6.	Are you ready to help and be involved in others' lives when they're feeling down?	Yes/No
7.	Do you find you're feeling sorry for yourself?	Yes/No
8.	Do you feel stuck in a rut and you think others can help?	Yes/No
9.	Do you think your phone is too silent?	Yes/No
10.	Are you ready to make space for others?	Yes/No

Circle your answers. Give yourself 1 point for each 'yes' answer in numbers 1, 4, 7, 8 and 9 and 1 point for each 'no' answer in numbers 2, 3, 5, 6 and 10. If you've got more than four points, you're thinking about yourself and not others.

Rule 1 – when making friends, ask them about themselves. Don't always talk about you. Most of us are more interested in ourselves and our families than in other people. If you want someone to like you, you need to be genuinely interested in that person.

Rule 2 – what you put out is what you get back. So you need to think about what type of friend you are. A good friend is someone who can share what's going on in their life – the good and the bad. They'll be genuinely interested and pleased when you succeed and sorry if things go wrong. They'll be able to suspend their needs while talking and being with you.

This can't be a one-way process. We all know the friends who are hard work and drain you because they only talk about themselves. If we're feeling needy, we can all fall into this trap. Observe yourself and keep remembering Rule 1: you reap what you sow! It may not be directly – you may turn out to be the mentor friend to someone else – but it's all about give and take.

We all have different friends for different things. As with everything in life, it's good to have a variety of friends; a breadth of friends widens your horizon. They're a fantastic source of knowledge and experience. You may want friends who are strong and supportive and whom you know will be there, with a cup of tea or glass of wine, when needed. Then there are those who are wise and full of sound advice.

People often talk about an older friend (yes, older even than you!) who they may have met at work or in a club. They may not be someone with whom you want to go to salsa classes but they're invaluable. Then there's the friend who's fun to be with, who makes you laugh and is up for anything. Some people enjoy a friendship with someone who's not afraid to give them honest feedback. Many people prefer to turn to a counsellor to satisfy this need.

Having a really close friend who's there for you through all life's ups and downs is a blessing. Make sure you value your relationship with your friends and cherish them. The more open and honest you are with each other, the deeper these relationships will become; some friends will grow closer to you than certain members of your family. But these relationships take time to build and nurture.

Think of all the different types of friends you have or would like to have. I know I pick up the phone to different people if I want to know what to read, what to wear, how to deal with an IT problem, how to manage my children; and I know different people call me for different things.

Rule 3 – be open to new people and don't be judgemental. Many of us have really close friends who we didn't connect with on first meeting. I had a client who told me that she'd known her closest friend for five years as a distant member of her social circle. One day, they'd met by chance in a local department store and got stuck in the lift for two hours. By the time they were rescued, they were great pals! I am not suggesting you need to go to those lengths but keep open to something developing. Don't leave it till circumstances force you to spend more time with someone. Actively seek out people if you feel you have something in common – otherwise, you, too, could be wasting five years of a rewarding relationship.

Rule 4 – go to places where like-minded people might be. If you're into sport, join a sports club; playing sport is a great way to meet people. Or, if you like wine, go on a wine course. Make a pact with yourself that you'll talk to at least one new person every time you go somewhere new. Most people find it hard to break the ice and get the conversation going. Think of a few opening questions you can ask someone. Remember, we all like someone who's interested in us. When you've made contact, follow it up. Take a contact number or arrange to see them at the next exercise class. Build on common experiences and suggest you do something together.

Rule 5 – if you don't seem to be getting anywhere, move on. There are lots of other people out there. Be clear how much time you have for others. Maintaining friendship takes time. If someone only hears from you when you're in a heap, they'll soon tire of you. Make sure you sometimes make the arrangements and not always leave it to them. If they keep saying they're busy, respect that. But not indefinitely. They might be signalling that they don't want this relationship to develop any further. If they're going through a bad patch, though, keep in touch without seeming to swamp them.

Rule 6 – remember that even your 'bestest' friend is only human. They'll at times make you sad or cross and sometimes appear selfish; they'll also bewilder you with what they say. But don't let a beautiful friendship slip away. Talk to them, sort out the problem and move on.

Rule 7 – talk about things that upset you and be honest. If, for whatever reason, the friendship has come to its natural end, don't sit at home nursing your wounds. Go out and make new friends. If you have friends who you feel you have grown away from or who sap your energy, don't run away from what's happening. Talk to them sensitively and see if you can build on the relationship. If not, you don't have to be hurtful: you can just slowly let it fade away.

Rule 8 – you talked about rekindling some of your previous friendships. My advice would be to take it slowly. They may be harbouring resentment that you distanced yourself when your job and family took priority. Let them say how they feel and then explain why you did what you did. Arrange to meet somewhere that's fun so you can begin to enjoy each other's company again rather than getting too intense. Above all, show genuine interest in them and their lives. Let them tell you what they've been up to first.

Sounds to me as if you're just about to embark on a really important journey, creating friends to share the next thirty years or so of your life. Having like-minded people of your own age to do this with will undoubtedly make it much better fun.

Q7 **I have brought my children up to be independent and I'm delighted they are – to a point! The problem is they've taken their independence too far and one plans to move to the other side of the world to take a good job. We've always been very close and I don't know if I can bear it. Sounds dramatic, I know, but that's how I feel. Have you any tips to help me with this? The way I'm behaving at the minute, they'll be running fast in the opposite direction!**

Well done, you, for doing what every parent dreams of doing: creating independent children who know their own mind and can make their own choices. But it's certainly true you can have too much of a good thing! It reminds me of the Lennon/McCartney song 'She's Leaving Home'. I remember hearing this and at the time wondering why anyone would make such a fuss when people left. It seemed to me then so natural and logical that people grow up, leave home and pursue their own lives.

What you're talking about has been labelled by psychologists the 'empty nest syndrome', but yours is with an added twist of distance. The term is commonly used to describe an emotional condition that can affect men and women (although more often women) when one or more of our children leave home. It can be particularly troubling when the last one leaves. I don't know how old your children are but, for many, the first time this feeling occurs is when children go to college. Someone once described to me their experience of dropping their son off at university for the first time. The experience was awash with emotion: adolescent fear and excitement mixed with parental anxiety and sorrow! Ninety-nine per cent of the time, the kids are over it by the next morning, the parents within a week or two. These feelings are very normal. Others, of course, find it a period of great freedom, a time they can at last think about themselves and their own needs and desires and not everyone else's. For most of us, it's a mixture of freedom and loss, pleasure and pain.

The time it really hits some mothers is when their children get married as that's a clear sign that you're no longer their most important person: they've chosen another. And that's hard to accept when you're used to being relied upon to be there when they've needed you for so long. Most children, particularly in the early stages after leaving home, believe that their parents are fossilised, waiting for the call or text to wake us up from our sleep to do whatever errand needs to be done. I remember hearing the late John Peel talk on *Home Truths* about his daughter losing her passport and money and all her identification when on holiday in Asia. The only way to get her home was for him or his wife to go out and get her. Never mind that they had important engagements! It made me wonder how many children would drop everything and come for us?

I think what you're saying is that your reactions feel too strong and they certainly aren't helpful to you or the child in question and probably not to any of the family. I'm sure that, while they're getting ready for their new life and involving you in the organisation and the plans, you'll feel quite stressed. At times like this, they can demand a lot of attention so that makes it even harder for you to prepare yourself for when they go.

And preparing yourself is essential. So what should you do? My first tip is to talk about what's happening. Tell your son or daughter how you feel. Calmly explain that you'll miss them and that the two of you need to think of ways to remain regularly in touch. There's nothing worse than making them feel guilty. We all know people who say they never felt able to leave home because of their parents' neediness; and that's not good for either party.

Very often during the build-up to the leaving, there'll be arguments or sulks because everyone's tense. Don't think for one minute your children don't have mixed feelings about leaving you. Make sure you talk things through and everyone understands each other. It's really important they don't go off with you or them in a huff! So be careful not to say things you'll regret.

Also, talk to your friends about how you feel. Don't complain to one child about the other, which will only prove divisive. Any remaining siblings will also be feeling sad about losing a pal and they'll need your support, too. Remember, you're all adults (albeit of different ages) and it's important to support each other.

Emails are an easy way to beat the time difference if a child has moved to the other side of the world. Buy yourself a webcam so you can see each other when you speak. It's not quite the same as having them in the same room but it's a lot better than not seeing them at all. It also means you can meet their friends and see where they live. Being familiar with their life will make you feel so much nearer to each other.

Make plans for when they go. Don't just sit at home looking at the four walls wondering what you're going to do. Arrange to see friends, go to exhibitions, the cinema and so on. Think of the things you've been putting off doing 'because of the children'. Start a new hobby or join a gym or evening classes or get out the easel and start painting!

If you're in a relationship, this may be the first time in twenty years you've been home alone with your partner. Plan some treats for the first few weeks so you can do good fun things together. It's important to take stock and look at what you both want in life and from your relationship as you enter a new chapter that doesn't focus on having children in the home.

If you're now single, this might be the right time to start looking for a new relationship. Whatever your circumstances, it's a good opportunity to make new friends based on shared interests and to widen your horizons.

The other side of the world is a long way away and expensive to get to. Start planning how you might go there one day. Put all your small coins in a jar each night; it's amazing how quickly they mount up. There are also great places to meet in the middle if your child lives in Australia, such as Hong Kong, Thailand or Bali, which would be fun to visit, cheaper to get to and which will give you the chance to see other bits of the world.

If you're really finding this tough, that it's unbearable and there's nothing to look forward to, I'd advise you to talk to your GP. He or she will be able to put you in touch with a counsellor who can help. In Section 2, Question 3, I explain EFT, a really helpful technique for managing difficult emotions. Why not give it a try? These changes in our children's lives coincide for most of us with changes in ourselves so don't feel bad if you need a little support along the way.

Finally, think about the actual leaving. What is the picture you want to remain with them? A sobbing mother or someone sad but able to get on with her own life? Really practise getting into the right frame of mind. You'll only have to wait till they've gone through the barrier and then you can cry! And, if you know you can't say goodbye without breaking down, say your good-byes at home and then text them when they're at the airport. Like most things, the anticipation is usually much worse than the reality.

Q8 **I have three children ranging from their late teens to mid-twenties. One hasn't left home yet and now the older two are back, having lived away for a bit. The eldest has recently broken up from a lovely partner after a long relationship. I've found their split really hard. I don't know if I should or shouldn't be in touch with her. He has just met someone new. My middle child has a partner who I don't think is at all suitable and my youngest has just started dating. How are you meant to manage your children's relationships?**

At the risk of sounding clichéd, parenting is a challenge. It's a relationship full of ambivalence. It gives us such warmth, love and joy but also angst, stress and upset. I've talked in Question 1, Section 4 about the fact that many of us will have adult relationships with our children for maybe thirty or forty years. These inter-generational relationships will be for many of us the longest and deepest of our lives. They are also probably the most tricky (bar your spouse/long-term partner).

The crucial difference, though, between our relationship with our children and our partners is that we choose our partners but not our children and they certainly didn't consciously choose their parents. And, unlike with our partners, we can't divorce our children, even if we sometimes fall out with them and become estranged.

It's the relationship that changes more than any other in our lives and one where we play so many different roles. We start out, rightly, making all the decisions for our children. We teach them how to become independent, we revel in the fact they can do things on their own, we wait for the day they're grown-up but as the person in the previous question pointed out – then they do it too well!

As parents, we start out on our journey with expectations of how our children are going to be. We have an end point for our endeavours and they don't always do it the way we've anticipated. They surprise us all the way through and sometimes with their choice of partner. When they're little, we may have had some influence on the friends they choose. This becomes less and less the case as they get older and, when they start dating, we have to let them make their own choices, hard as it may be.

It's very often helpful, when trying to work out how to behave, to think about our own experiences. Take a few quiet minutes and cast your mind back to when you brought home your first boyfriend or girlfriend.

EXERCISE: MY EARLY RELATIONSHIPS

1. What was it like?

2. How did your parents behave?

3. What did they do well?

4. What did they do badly?

5. What would you have liked them to have done differently?

6. What did they talk to you about after your partner left?

7. How did they respond when you split up?

8. How were they when you brought the next boyfriend/girlfriend home?

9. Ask yourself the same questions for each new person
   they met. You should now have the start of a list of what
   works and what doesn't.

The way that we live now means that our children will be exploring
new relationships while they're still living at home. Your children are part of what has been termed by the sociologists the
'boomerang' generation, those born between approximately 1978
and 1989. Many more young people go away to university or
college than used to. They often move out at that stage, come
back to work out what they want to do next and pay off loans,
move out and flat-share or move in with partners and return if
the relationship ends, stay a while and then off they go again.
Unlike with previous generations, our older children maintain their
own social and professional lives while living under our roof and
see themselves as independent people who happen to live at home.

When we were young, our early boy- or girlfriends were met by
our parents but deeper relationships generally started while we
were living independently and the partners were then introduced
at a point when the relationship was becoming serious. Today's
lifestyle has meant that many parents are faced with getting
to know their children's partners at a much earlier stage and
more intimately.

Managing ourselves in relation to our adult children and their
relationships is tricky. At times it will feel as though you're
walking on eggshells if you want your children to be actively
part of your life and you a part of theirs.

First thing to remember is that every new boy or girlfriend introduced is your child's choice. You and they will have no idea
whether this will be the one still in all your lives when you're
in your eighties. It's therefore not a casual meeting. It's not like
being introduced to someone at a friend's house and deciding

they aren't your cup of tea and never seeing them again. We all know people who say, 'I've never liked my mother-in-law,' a relationship that got off to a bad start and never fully recovered.

Your children will see their partners as an extension of themselves. They're the people they've chosen to fall in love with. So never judge them harshly as this will push your child into a defensive position. A further concern for many mothers of boys is expressed in the saying, 'A son's a son 'til he gets him a wife, but a daughter's a daughter the rest of your life.' The fear is that, when a son gets a permanent partner, buys his own home and has children, it will be his wife's mother who's most involved and especially when the first child arrives.

Depending on your family values, you can decide what your children are allowed to do in your house and you need to make this clear. If it's all right for them to sleep together, fine; if not, that's fine, too. But make sure they're aware of the ground rules in advance. Everyone has their own code of behaviour. The last thing you want to do is make guests feel uncomfortable or unwelcome.

It's great if you get on well with your child's partner but it's important to remember that it's their relationship. It's not unusual for parents to fall 'in love' with their child's new partner to a greater or lesser extent. Often, this is because it gives us an opportunity to relive our own youth and remember those early heady days of a hot romance. Sometimes, however, it can make us envious of their relationships or sad that ours is somehow lacking. Many people have also said to me that, even when they really like the partner, they never get the intimate chats with their child they used to. That's probably going to be especially true at the start of the new relationship but there's nothing to be done about it.

Melanie Klein (1882–1960) was an Austrian-born British psychoanalyst and one of the founders of psychodynamics. She devised
therapeutic techniques for children that influenced methods of
childcare and childrearing. She coined a new psychological term,
'projective identification', in 1946. It refers to a psychological
process whereby a person will disown a facet of themselves
and project it on to another person. The second person picks up the
projection (unconsciously) and behaves as though he or she actually has those thoughts, feelings or beliefs. What tends to get
projected are painful feelings or difficult or unpleasant beliefs or
ideas about ourselves that we find hard to handle. The bound-
aries between the two people and their feelings can become
blurred as a result.

This is something that we all do unconsciously in intimate
relationships. In mature relationships, the two people begin to
identify what feelings each person is carrying on behalf of the
other. ('How come I'm always the person who's angry/anxious/
depressed in this relationship?') Make sure that, if your child's
partner triggers a negative feeling in you, you don't dump something you don't want on to your child, making them feel confused
and angry. Mother-in-law jokes may or may not be funny but
they're based on reality!

Not only is it hard when your child meets someone special; it
can be just as hard when they split up. If your child's partner
falls out of love with them it can be particularly hard for the
parent to take. It feels like a personal affront. We all fundament-
ally want our children to be loved and adored by all. Your role
is not to tell your child how horrid the person is but to be there
for them, just listening. If you develop an independent relationship with the former partner and you want to continue seeing
them, this is something you and your child need to discuss. In
the end, it needs to be your child's decision. But be careful to
choose an appropriate time when they've finished grieving.

Whatever you do, it's important to remember that they're no longer part of the family so your relationship with the former partner needs to be independent.

If it is your child who's caused the split, don't take the ex-partner's side against your child, even if you do think your child behaved badly. That's a separate issue. Your child needs to see you as their supporter. As long as you pursue your desire to maintain a good relationship with your child, you'll find a way to steer yourself through the vicissitudes of a broken heart.

And I think even those of you who aren't planning on introducing a new person into your family would do well to read Section 3, Question 9 as it deals with the other side of the coin.

Q9 I'm about to become a grandmother. I'm both thrilled and panicked. My mother devoted her later years to her family which included lots of childcare. I'm 57, have a full-time job and a busy social life. But I find myself unable to explain this to my 28-year-old daughter. I devoted so much time to my children when they were growing up. I now want a bit of time for me! Am I being selfish? And how do I tell her?

No, you're not being selfish. A very significant change in our society over the last thirty years has been the increased number of women who now work either full or part time and remain working well into their sixties or beyond. Although we've accepted this on one level and have goals that are different from our parents' generation, we've retained some of the old traditions and possibly given our children the expectation we'll be like our parents – in other words, old-fashioned grandparents.

What you're asking is how do we embrace this really special role and yet maintain our independence? When you become a grandparent, you'll be joining the other approximately 13 million grandparents in the UK. One in every three people are grandparents by the time they reach 50; by 54, it's one in two! One in two grandparents has a living parent and over a third of grandparents under the age of 60 still have a dependant child of their own living at home. (Source: www.grandparentsplus.org.uk.)

Research done by Geoff Dench, Professor of Sociology at Middlesex University, who has a special interest in grandparenting, states in *Grandparenting in Britain: A Baseline Study* that almost 40 per cent of grandparents would like to have a life free from too many family duties, while 64 per cent think that a government subsidy should be offered to grandparents who are involved in regular childcare. So, in no way are you alone. The economic demands that many young people face with steep mortgages and the high cost of childcare have meant that many have turned to their families for help with the grandchildren.

With the changes in the retirement age, many women will need to carry on working longer, which will cut down on the number of active grandparents at home with time on their hands.

Becoming a grandparent is a landmark step. Life will never be the same again. As you say, the prospect fills you with a mixture of emotions: joy, anticipation, apprehension and sadness for the passing of time. Your grandchild will create a new generation in the family. Each of us has our own picture of what a grandmother is like. Often, we remember them in their later years either as delightful, frail, old people or as cantankerous and difficult. Neither picture fits us, of course! If we still have a parent alive, it just doesn't seem possible that we could now be grandparents.

What it does do is make us confront our own ageing and remind us of the cycle of life and the passing of generations.

Becoming a grandparent is certainly not a step you consciously chose; no one asked if this was the right time for *you*. From what you say, it isn't that you don't want to be a grandmother – just not necessarily yet. I don't know from what you say if your daughter has told you she is planning for you to be actively involved when the baby is born or if this is an assumption on your part. Relationships built up over the years like yours and your daughter's will have evolved habitual patterns. If so, the two of you need to look at how you'll change these habits. And now is the perfect moment to begin those discussions. (See Section 4, Questions 1 and 3.) It won't be easy but it's worth it.

You raise another of what I call the hidden 50+ questions, the ones that don't make us sound perfect. What you're grappling with is the kind of grandparent you want to be. I'm sure you remember when you had your first child: although you may have wanted advice from your parents or in-laws when you asked, it never felt the same when they offered it unsolicited. It never felt like they really understood and, anyway, they had brought us up differently.

We didn't follow Truby King, childcare guru for mothers in the forties and early fifties, or Doctor Spock in the fifties and sixties. We followed Penelope Leach and we knew best! This will be true for your daughter, too, who'll have her own childcare guru. But some things never change. You'll always be your daughter's mother but not the baby's mother; your role will be different and you are not the prime carer. This doesn't mean you won't worry when the child is sick or miserable at school. And, just by being there, you'll be able to offer something really special that your grandchild can get from no one else.

I think it would be helpful for you to think about the following questions. Once you know the answers, you'll be in a good position to talk to your daughter. Ask her to do the same thing so you have both done some pre-thinking.

EXERCISE: HOW READY AM I TO BECOME A GRANDPARENT?

Ask yourself:

1. How much involvement do I want?

2. Will my partner want the same amount of involvement?

3. Do I want to look after the baby regularly? During the day? At weekends? In my home? In their home? Do I want to babysit?

4. How much do I think I'll be needed (base this on how often you and your daughter see each other now) and is this what I want?

5. How much time do I have to look after the baby?

6. How do I want my relationship with my grandchild to be?

7. What do I want to tell them of our family history so it doesn't get lost in the passing of the generations, and how am I going to do this?

8. How can I be a positive influence in my grandchild's life and make a real difference?

9. How am I going to shift from the role I know to one

where it isn't my place to say anything unless asked and then to do so gently?

10. How am I going to manage when the choices the parents make aren't the ones I would make?

11. And how might any of this affect my travel plans?

Grandparenting, like parenting, doesn't come with a manual. There are now more books and papers available on the subject than there were (see the Resource List) but it still involves intuition, trial and error and accepting that you may make some mistakes.

Here are a few tips on making it work:

- Remember, they're the parents, not you!

- The grandchildren have two parents, one of whom isn't your child and may have different values and ideas.

- Stay on good terms with your children and their partners: they're the gateway to your grandchildren.

- Wait to be asked – don't offer an opinion – and remind yourself how insecure you were as a parent and how easily you heard well-intended remarks as criticism.

- Never tell your grandchildren their parents are wrong.

- Agree with your daughter what you can and can't do so no one is disappointed with each other.

- Don't assume that your child wants you to do the childcare.

- Don't expect the new parents to have time to worry about

you and how you feel in your role – they've got enough on their plate.

There are lots of ways to be a grandparent and lots of roles that don't involve doing the childcare. Barusch and Steen (1996) call grandparents 'keepers of the community' because they pass on and interpret knowledge of events and people. Offering this kind of input can only be done by you. And yes, offer to help out in a crisis but don't be expected to ask to pitch in every day. And, finally, I think the fact that you pose this question in the first place shows you're already on the right track to make it work for you, your daughter and the new baby.

Q10 **My son has the knack of making me feel old and useless. This has come to a head over his children. I know all the rules about what you should and shouldn't say but I'm worried about some of the behaviour I see in my granddaughter and grandson. How can I just sit by and watch? Or am I really past my sell-by date?**

I think there are two issues here: one is your relationship with your son and daughter-in-law and the other is your feeling of being old and useless. It's interesting that you've linked the two together. I'm sure there are many older people who feel 'past their sell-by date' who don't have grandchildren! In a world which in the last fifty years has idolised the young, it's inevitable that those of us who aren't young will at times feel past our sell-by date.

So your son makes you feel old and past it. No, you feel old and past it and he's touched your Achilles heel. No one knows better how to hurt us than our nearest and dearest. It is the easiest form of defence when we feel attacked. My hunch is that, when you've talked to your son about his children, you've made him feel adolescent which is promptly how he behaved. We pick up insults and find them hurtful when they contain a grain of truth.

None of us like to acknowledge we aren't as up-to-date as our children. But the fact is that we were brought up at a different time in a different way and by different people. Each generation has to learn from its own mistakes; we can't protect them from this and nor should we. We can offer support and suggestions but that's as far as it goes.

I expect some of what you think about childrearing is past its sell-by date while other bits are spot on. (See the previous question.) Your children will think some of what their parents did was good and want to repeat it while choosing to do other things the opposite way. What I expect happened was that, when you were talking to your son and daughter-in-law, what they heard you tell them was that they were doing parenting wrong. They didn't hear you focus on the specific behaviour you were concerned about. Understandably, they didn't like it and felt criticised and put down.

As a generation, I think we're guilty of fantasising about how well we relate to our children. The reality is that we'll always be the parent in this relationship and we'll always be seen like that by our kids. As they grow older, this relationship will become more blurred but, at moments of stress, our offspring will revert to their child position, which will force us back into our roles as parents.

Just because your son and his wife don't agree with you doesn't make you useless. It's simply that you have a different opinion. I think Section 3, Question 1 which discusses self-confidence would be useful for you to look at. You might try the exercises if you feel you need a bit of a boost. It's important that you find a different way to relate to your son about issues that concern you. To refresh yourself about the dos and don'ts of good grandparenting, see the previous question.

Your question brought to mind a situation that happened to me many years ago. I was walking down the street with a friend who was attending to her younger child who was in a buggy. At that point, her three-year-old son decided to cross the road by himself. I instinctively shouted at him to come back. This alerted my friend who pulled him out of the road, narrowly escaping being run down.

To my surprise, my friend then turned on me and berated me for talking to her son like that. She then decided she would no longer come back to my house for tea and flounced off leaving me bewildered since I'd just prevented a potentially serious accident. Later that evening, she called round with a bunch of flowers to say thank you for saving her child. She explained that her maternal protective instincts had flared up and all she saw in the heat of the moment was an attack on her child.

Try the exercise below to help you find a new approach in dealing with your children's parenting skills.

EXERCISE: PRACTISING SKILLS

1. Find a quiet, comfortable space where you can sit and think back to when someone said something negative about your child or your childrearing.

2. Think of five situations – it might be the teacher who wasn't impressed with your son, the friend whose parent said your child behaved badly – and then write them down.

3. Now divide them into two categories: one where you still disagree with what was said; the other where you came to believe the negative feedback was useful. Focus on these events and use the association technique discussed in Section 1, Question 3 to really get in touch with your feelings.

4. Having 'relived' these, did you find there were times you felt OK when told about the problem and you were grateful for the advice? If there are, that's great because you will have experienced some excellent communication and in spite of the person saying something that you might have found difficult they managed to offer good advice without making you defensive.

5. Make a note of what they did to help you listen and accept their words. How did they talk to you? What non-verbal messages did they give?

6. If there weren't any, go back to one of the not-so-good situations and this time disassociate from it and run it as a movie. Whilst watching, tell the critical advice-giver how to give you the advice in a way you could hear it. Now associate in again imagining they have learnt your lessons and are doing it the 'right' way for you. How do you feel now? Jot down the techniques.

7. Now think about something that you wish someone had said to you about your child or your relationship with them but didn't – for example, that you were spending so much time on the naughty one that the other was getting left out, or that you didn't play with them enough because you were worried about the housework. Every parent will have made mistakes with their children.

8. Now ask yourself some soul-searching questions about the advice you're giving your son and daughter-in-law and be truthful about the answers:

   a) Am I offering my views on things that are a matter of opinion – the time a child should go to bed, what they should eat, which type of school they should go to and so on?

   b) Am I offering advice based on the childrearing methods of my time?

   c) Am I offering advice because I don't like that sort of behaviour?

   d) Am I offering advice about the way my son is managing a situation because I think I know best?

   e) Do I genuinely believe that my grandchild will be physically or psychologically damaged if nothing is done?

In my opinion, you really need to consider your role as a grandparent and look again at the dos and don'ts. If the answer is 'yes' to Question 8(e), then you have a duty to say something with regard to your grandchildren. We've all been in situations where our own concerns about the reaction we might get stops us saying things that need to be said.

It reminds me of a client who was a speech therapist and concerned about her niece whom she thought had a hearing problem. She felt it was impossible to tell her brother and sister-in-law as they would immediately tell her she was being a clever-clogs professional. Having carefully rehearsed what she was going to say, though, she finally voiced her concerns. Her brother and his wife weren't happy and said all the things she'd expected but she stayed confident and true to herself. The rest of the evening was frosty.

A few weeks later, her sister-in-law called and said she'd made an appointment with the audiologist and a minor problem had been discovered which fortunately could be sorted very easily. If they'd waited for the routine clinic appointment in eight months, their daughter would have missed out on a crucial period for language learning which might have affected her all her life.

If the situation is of concern, then it needs to be talked about. It may well not be easy and, as you'll have discovered in the exercise above, it has to be handled sensitively and with forethought and planning. The following tips will help you to discuss things and reduce the likelihood of confrontation:

- Remind yourself what works and what doesn't when talking about difficult issues.

- Find a chance to talk when the grandchildren are not there and everyone has time and isn't stressed – sometimes, going for a walk can be a good idea. If your son and daughter-in-law think you're undermining them in front of their child, it can only end in tears.

- Talk about the issues away from the event and not while it's happening.

- Keep yourself in the 'adult' position. (See Section 4, Question 1.)

- Tell them how difficult it is for you all to talk about situations where you have concerns.

- Let them know you think they're doing a fantastic job and that it's far from easy being a parent.

- Remind them that you know who is the child's parent.

- Tell them that, when they were little, even though you didn't like people criticising you, at times it was helpful.

- Ask them a question about why they're doing something and enter into a dialogue about it. Be open and give and take in the discussion.

- Never forget that it's their decision.

Follow these guidelines and you're much more likely to maintain good long-lasting, inter-generational relationships. You might also find these tips useful in other relationships when you're of the opinion as to how others should do things.

Q11 I suddenly feel grown-up and old. I am the most senior member of my family alive! I feel as though all my choices have gone and I'm scared. What can I do about this?

I recently went to a funeral of an elderly woman. She was the youngest of six and had been the last living member of her generation for a number of years. Her eldest niece was in quite a dither. She said she felt as though the whole responsibility for the family had now been thrown at her, that she'd been handed the baton without any discussion and didn't quite know what to do. But, by the time she had left the wake, she'd organised a family party so that everyone kept in touch.

Besides being sad, there's something very unsettling about a parent's death, even if we ourselves are in our fifties or sixties.

Part of us feels that our parents are meant to be there for us for ever, giving us unconditional love and attention, praising our successes, soothing our brows when we're distressed and standing up for us whatever we do – in short, being there for us when we need them. We hold on to that illusion long past our youth and who could say, hand on heart, that they don't want their mum when they're feeling low?

The inner child's dreams are shattered when that parent has gone. You feel lost and alone. You think to yourself, 'Well, if there's no one there to parent me, I must be the grown-up. And, as grown-ups are seen as old, I must be old!' Your question reminded me of my own mother when I was about fifteen and she was in her mid-forties, sitting on the floor in the middle of the sitting-room, sobbing when her father died and saying over and over again, 'I'm an orphan.'

When talking with a group of women recently, it struck me how those who were fortunate enough to still have two healthy parents when they were well into their fifties still felt young. They were much less concerned with many of the issues associated with ageing. They rarely thought about it and the reality was that, in their family, they were not seen as old. Those with either one parent still alive or neither felt they had had to face lots of issues to do with ageing and it reminded them of their own mortality!

Several women have said to me that, because they now visit their lonely and ill elderly parents, the issue of age is with them all the time. If a parent is ill or has dementia, they seem to take a lot of space in people's minds even if they are not physically looking after them. This constant reminder gnaws away at one's own self-image. However, it is those with no parents left alive who now feel they're the grown-ups. (This happens whatever age you are when you lose both parents.) The loss of both parents shifts you up a generation; you're the older generation now. There's no one for you to fall back on and that can feel a bit scary. You have to take on the responsibility for your own ageing, knowing you're next in line.

Going back to your question, it seems to me that your feelings are very normal and understandable. What needs to be dealt with is the feeling of being scared and that you have no choices. I don't know if you've recently been bereaved. My hunch is that that's probably the case and you've lost sight of your own future. The reality, though, is that all the choices you had before are still there. Creating choices is looked at in Section 1, Question 1. I would suggest that you look at that and follow the exercise.

You talk about being fearful. Fear can be paralysing. We feel panicked and stuck. When we're frightened or alarmed by either an external factor or something in our head, a physiological response is triggered in our body. This is known as the flight or fight response. If you were to meet a tiger on a street corner, you'd know to run! When we perceive danger it stimulates our autonomic nervous system – a second unconscious automatic nervous system – to release noradrenalin and adrenalin itself. These in turn tell other parts of our body to react so our pupils dilate, our heart rate increases, our breathing becomes faster and shallower, insulin is released into our blood system, our blood pressure rises, our palms sweat, blood is diverted away from our digestive system and skin and our muscles tense.

Simultaneously, stress activates our pituitary gland releasing ACTH (adrenocorticotrophic hormone) into our system. This tells the adrenal glands to get busy and to produce cortisol, which causes stress-related physical reactions.

Fear is useful if it is alerting us to danger, giving us an opportunity to avoid it. However, our bodies don't always know how to distinguish between real danger and imagined threats. If you have this reaction when no physical action is needed – for example, feeling nervous when you're at a party and don't know anyone – you have no choice but to suppress it. What follows is a build-up of anxiety which is no good for your health or emotional state. It leaves you panicked and without the ability to make choices.

There are some very simple techniques that can help us to reduce anxiety and get us back into a state of equilibrium.

EXERCISE: EMERGENCY RELAXATION TECHNIQUE

When you're getting really worked up:

1. Say, 'Stop!' firmly to yourself – aloud if the situation permits, mentally if not.

2. Breathe in, becoming aware of your jaw and shoulders as you do so. Breathe out slowly, making the exhalation longer than the inhalation, allowing your shoulders and jaw to relax as you do so. Mentally say to yourself, 'Let go.'

3. Breathe in, focusing your awareness on your chest, arms and hands. Breathe out slowly, relaxing your chest, arms and hands as you do so. Mentally say, 'Let go.'

4. Breathe in, focusing your awareness on your stomach muscles, thighs and buttocks. Breathe out slowly allowing your stomach muscles, thighs and buttocks to relax as you do so. Mentally say, 'Let go.'

In the time it takes to breathe in and out three times, you can become aware of tension in the body and let it go. If your breathing is very shallow or you are panting, try cupping one or both your hands over your nose and mouth so that you're breathing in your expelled air. This alerts the breathing centre in the brain to slow down. Be aware only of breathing out slowly; the body will automatically breathe in for you. Mental stress will lessen when you relax the muscles and slow the breathing.

EXERCISE: EMERGENCY ACTIVITIES TECHNIQUE

1. Get up and move around. Our mental and physical states are inextricably linked. You have all this chemical activity in your body and it needs an outlet. By taking physical action, you can change your mental state very quickly.

2. Stand up and sit down five times. Concentrate on your body. Be aware of what you're doing.

3. Now walk briskly either on the spot or go for a walk, really focusing on what you're doing.

4. Take five really deep breaths and focus on your breathing. As you exhale, see yourself breathing away any negative feelings.

5. Summon up a mental picture that makes you feel good. Put in some music and some movement. Have this picture ready to register on your mind whenever you become anxious. As soon as you're thinking positive thoughts, different chemicals are triggered and the body relaxes.

6. Now begin to focus on the issue in hand, i.e. your fear at being a 'grown-up'. Think of one tiny thing you'd like to

do – start by making a list of all the things you've always wanted to achieve. Then sit down and work at how to do it. Start with one small activity. Success breeds success.

If you practise these techniques, you'll find that your feelings of fear will dissipate and that you'll be able once again to make the choices that are good for you.

❧ Section Five ❧

You're Never Too Old to ...
Have Money and a Career

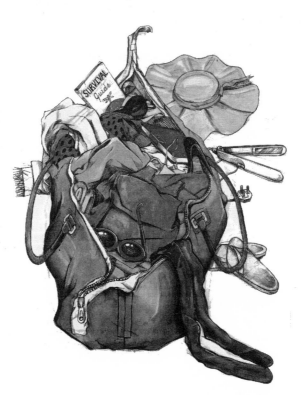

S o many of the people I have spoken to find themselves at 50+ not in the financial position they had expected to be in. Many who believed that, by the time they were in their fifties and certainly sixties, they would have paid for their homes and be picking up a pension based on their final salary are finding that things have changed.

As a result of divorce and maintenance payments, many people are still paying for mortgages, or renting property for themselves and ex-spouses, that they did not expect to be doing at this stage of their lives. Alongside this, pension funds are depleted, while people's welfare is very dependent on the global economy and the housing market. Little wonder so many individuals feel trapped, unable to see how they'll ever be able to stop working.

Others, by contrast, have no financial concerns but aren't the slightest bit ready to give up work. Some like what they do and they want to continue on the same path; others are ready for a fresh challenge and want to develop a new career or business. Retirement for them is a long way off.

Q I'm the oldest in my office. I feel past my sell-by date and that I should retire but I'm not even 60. No one listens to me any more. What would I do with myself? I've so many ideas of the things I could do at work but they seem to fall on stony ground.

You do sound sorry for yourself and I must say, that often isn't very appealing in a grown woman! I know it's something that we all do at times but, if you're walking around your office with that attitude, I'm not surprised no one's listening. When we feel sorry for ourselves, we tend to think about 'me, myself and I' and little else.

As I'm sure you know, when someone becomes self-absorbed, we lose interest. That happens whatever our age. If you're older than a lot of your colleagues, you have to learn how to speak the same language so you're on their wavelength.

I think I may have just the answer – two ideas from two different schools of thought on how we behave and think. Once you've mastered these two, you'll be amazed how much notice people take of you.

Let's start with an idea from Neuro-Linguistic Programming (NLP) whose founder members, Richard Bandler and John Grindler, were very interested in how people communicated. They happened to be in California teaching at the university when some of the great therapists were working and developing their fields. Fritz Perls (Gestalt therapy), Virginia Satir (family therapy), Milton Eriksson (hypnosis) and Carl Rogers (Rogerian counselling). These therapists worked very differently and had amazing results, but all of them had to persuade people to open up and talk about intimate and painful matters.

To make this possible, Bandler and Grindler studied both the non-verbal communication and the language used. What they noticed was that, when people are asked a question, they move their eyes as if they're searching for the information in their brain. Everything we experience is stored in our brain and, when it's triggered by a word, sound, picture, smell or taste, the information goes into our consciousness and we remember the event. They observed that, when we're looking for visual information, we look up; when we're looking for auditory information, our eyes stay horizontal; and when we're picking up an emotion or having an internal dialogue with ourselves, we look down.

Don't believe me? Just for a minute, try multiplying 97 by 48 without the use of pen, paper or calculator. I bet you 'wrote it in your head', looking up to get the picture. It's the same with spelling. Try to spell a difficult word without writing it down and the only way is to 'write it in your head' and read it off. I find myself scanning my virtual list at the top of my head when I leave the shopping list at home. If you still don't believe me, find a friend to do the following exercise with you. Ask them to ask you the questions and observe where your eyes go and then do it with them.

Do you remember being asked to stand up and say your tables at school? I was probably seven and got as far as 8x7 and then faltered. So I looked up to bring the page into my head and the teacher shouted at me and told me the answer wasn't on the ceiling (it was on mine!). I looked down, got in touch with my feelings and started to cry. I was then sent out for being a baby! Happily, one thing that has improved over the years is the understanding of children and the way they learn.

EXERCISE: EYE ACCESSING CUES

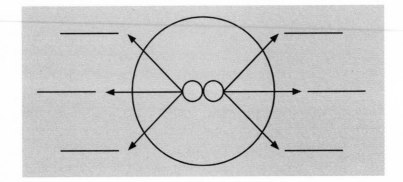

Ask each question, one at a time. Watch the eye movement and write the question number in the appropriate place.

1. Picture a friend's face.

2. Imagine your bedroom painted pink with blue spots.

3. Hear the sound of a favourite piece of music.

4. Hear the noise of a horse neighing.

5. Think of the feeling of silk on your skin.

6. Ask yourself what you'll do after you've finished this exercise.

Each one of us has a preferred way of thinking and processing information so, if you're a visual person and I present my ideas to you using visual words, you'll be interested. If I use auditory words, you might not be. Very often, when we're pitching an idea to someone, we only have a minute so we have to find a way to get their immediate attention.

We interact and gather information from the world using our five senses:

V	Visual	*seeing*	A	Auditory	*hearing*
K	Kinaesthetic	*feeling*	O	Olfactory	*smelling*
G	Gustatory	*tasting*			

We tend to use some senses more than others. We may have general preferences, and use some senses for specific jobs such as photography (V), perfumery (O) and so on. Through these five senses, we re-present the world to ourselves internally. These are consequently called representational systems. The language we use offers clues to our sensory processing.

Below is a list of words that might help you:

VISUAL		AUDITORY		KINAESTHETIC	
See	Look	Hear	Say	Feel	Touch
View	Picture	Listen	Click	Grab	Pressure
Vision	Focus	Sound	Resonate	Pull	Handle
Colourful	Scan	Tone	Rhythm	Grasp	Texture
Outlook	Perspective	Accent	Harmony	Rub	Heavy
Insight	Clear	Music	Tune in	Sticky	Firm

VISUAL		AUDITORY		KINAESTHETIC	
Reflect	Murky	Call	Clash	Rough	Uptight
Sparkle	Bright	Loud	Discordant	Smooth	Pushy
Highlight	Transparent	Whisper	Echo	Gritty	Sting

Because these information-processing modes have become part of our way of life, we no longer notice them; mostly, that's fine. However, when communication is just not working, it's extremely useful to notice how other people make sense of the world. If things aren't flowing, it's likely that their system is very different from yours. The language people use is a clue as to how they're processing information. If you're operating in different modes – visual, auditory and kinaesthetic – you're going to find it difficult to see 'eye-to-eye'. Or, to put it another way, things won't 'sound harmonious' or 'feel all of a piece' to them. Adopt their style and you'll find that communication flows much more smoothly.

Then there's the Herrmann® Thinking Preferences, another metaphoric model of how the brain operates. Created by Ned Herrmann, he combined the Triune Brain model of Paul McLean which divides the brain into the outer rational cerebellum, the middle limbic, more emotional part and the reptilian, more instinctive part with the Left/Right Brain Hemisphere Theory of Roger Sperry to form a model of the human brain with four quarters: two halves of the cerebral system and two halves of the limbic system. The four quadrants are A-logical, B-organised, C-interpersonal, and D-imaginative. Ned Herrmann's theory is based on the fact that there is likely to be one or more dominant quadrants which become our habitual ways of thinking and where we revert to when under stress, but we are all capable of any of these types of thinking. Herrmann developed a validated assessment used to determine thinking preferences, the HBDI®, Herrmann Brain Dominance Instrument. The diagram below is a representation of the model provided by Herrmann International.

Whole Brain™ Mode

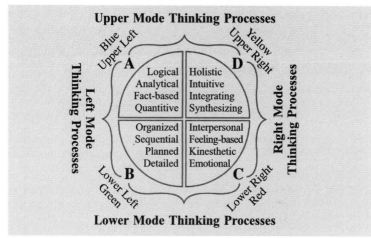

Quadrant A is concerned with intellectual processing which is structured and systematic. If you had a predisposition for this quadrant you would probably tackle problem-solving in a step-by-step manner. You would be interested in, and include an account of, facts, figures, statistics and other tangibles in your thinking, and you would have supporting data or examples of precedent to back up your conclusions. This style is logical, analytical and rational; you would use it for feasibility studies, making critical assessments and any task that needs rigorous and focused thinking. You need Quadrant A for financial, mathematical and technical issues. You may dislike any emotional, woolly, unsubstantiated type of thinking.

Quadrant B is structured in a practical and procedural way. If this were your predisposition, you would be inclined towards organisation, reliability, efficiency, order and discipline. You would prioritise tasks and work in a systematic and sequential manner and you would manage time efficiently, completing all your tasks in the time allowed. You would be methodical and attentive to details, and you would be skilled at operational planning and the implementation of schemes and projects. You would like administration and maintaining systems and procedures, but dislike chaos and confusion and be very skilled in making order out of a situation. You may be cautious, controlled and planned; you may also tend to explain things in minute detail.

Quadrant C is concerned with emotions. Your natural bent would be towards feelings and interpersonal matters. You would tend to be attracted to people and have an ability to relate quickly and easily with others. People would be likely to tell you about themselves, as you would have good interpersonal skills and an innate ability to create rapport and be easy with conversation. You would use your intuition and have a feel for the answer, and would often be heard to say you had a gut feeling or hunch about something. You would enjoy being with people and talking to them and, when problem-solving, would be concerned about the effect the decision would have on others. You may dislike being asked to pinpoint the facts.

Quadrant D is concerned with more abstract thinking. You would often handle several thoughts at the same time. When problem-solving, you would tend to look at several aspects at the same time, creating pictures and models in your head and making spontaneous conclusions. You would tend to be a lateral thinker and be imaginative, innovative and have original ideas. You may dislike detail and prefer thinking about the big picture. You may find it difficult or frustrating when completing tasks as you would prefer to be on to the next thing.

These different approaches to thinking are important because they'll help you consider how this affects your communication with people. If work colleagues think differently from you, they may not find it easy to follow what you're suggesting. The easiest communication is between people who are dominant in the same quadrant while it is also helpful if people share dominances in the left-brain or the right brain. People with two cerebral or two limbic scores often cope well together, while those with a high disposition to diametrically opposed quadrants are the most likely to clash.

Once you and you colleagues understand each other and find a common language, you'll hopefully realise that they're not intentionally trying to wind you up; they are just doing it their way, which might not be your preferred style. Use both thinking models given as a guide to ensure every idea is seen as golden and I don't think you'll give retirement a second thought for quite a while!

Q2 **I'm 56 and sadly not in the financial position I planned. I'm sick with worry about money. If I live till I'm 90, I'll be in the poor house. I have a minimal pension which won't begin to keep me. I have no choice but to retire from my job shortly. I have so much experience and knowledge but have no idea how to use this to my advantage. My children say they'll see me right but that would be intolerable.**

You're certainly not alone with this worry although it may at times feel like it. Talking about our finances to our friends and family is still for many a taboo subject. We can present to the world an image that all is well when internally we're worried and with no one to talk to. As a life coach, I've spoken to many people who feel as you do. Some say that the fear of poverty at times has paralysed their thinking so they find themselves holding on to a job that no longer suits them or setting up a new business without enough research. (Over-worrying is not at all helpful, so please look at Section 6, Question 5.)

Recent research studies (www.dwp.gov.uk) have concluded that the majority of people in their fifties and sixties don't have adequate financial provision for their old age. Some 56 per cent of working-age people in the UK expected their retirement to last at least twenty years. Only 7 per cent thought they'd be in retirement for less than ten years. In 2002, just over half of people of working age thought a weekly income of less than £250 would be adequate to live on if they retired today and many are now realising this is not the case.

This is yet another area where the baby boomers are pioneers. The state pension has not kept up with the cost of living and every day we read about both the government and companies cutting back final salary pensions. Most people haven't saved sufficient sums.

This generation of women of 50 to 65 is sandwiched between those who've already reached retirement age (and many of whom never expected to work once they were married) and our children's generation who were brought up by us to expect that women would work full time and achieve equal success to men as well as have a family.

We were also brought up to expect the reward of a secure retirement at 60, so, when our expectations don't meet the reality, managing this 'expectations' gap is one of the hardest challenges to face. The idea of an impoverished old age is a bleak one.

So why has this happened? Some of us took career breaks to have children and didn't pay the full insurance stamp in the meantime and therefore will not receive a full pension. Many of us are divorced and some widowed. Divorce in particular has played a big part in our financial standing.

The over-fifties divorce rate is soaring. One in seven people aged between 50 and 64 is now divorced. There is also evidence that older people are divorcing for a second time, which adds to the financial burden – something, of course, that can apply equally to men.

Half of all women over 65 now live by themselves, which is not what they were conditioned to expect. As a result of divorce, many women are paying for mortgages or renting property and that they did not plan to be doing at this stage of their lives. All of this understandably leads to worry about finances in our old age. Most of us, like you, do not want to be a burden on their children. I am making the assumption that you're on your own, widowed or divorced, as you don't mention a partner, so you have to sort out this problem yourself.

I think there are two issues to explore here: one is how to feel more positive about your situation so you can create something new, and the other is how to make the money to finance your lifestyle.

How we feel about our financial situation is as important as the situation itself. If you let yourself spiral into a panic, you'll not find a solution. Before you do anything to rectify the specific money issue, take yourself off to a quiet spot and write down ten things you've got that you cherish – your children, memories of holidays and so on. Now ask yourself, 'Would I give up any of these for a bit more money?' Even if the answer is 'yes' for one or two, I don't suppose they'll be in the top five. So, remember: you're rich in life, if not in pennies. Focusing on what you've got rather than what you haven't will immediately make you feel better.

Something I've noticed is that, when people worry about money, their problems seem bigger than they really are. Find a professional financial advisor to talk to. They'll help you to work out your shortfall and how best to maximise any financial assets you have. You'll then have real figures to work with and not fantasy ones that only fuel your anxieties. For those of us fortunate enough to own our homes, that will always offer some source of additional income. Even if you rent, you may well be able to live somewhere smaller and cheaper.

The reality is that the majority of us will have less to live on when we are retired than when we are working. If we want to go on doing the things we've always done, we'll need to supplement our income. You said that you had to retire but, with the new pension regulations, you can draw a pension and work. Lots of businesses are now actively looking to employ older workers as they're seen as reliable and experienced. You may find it helpful to explore some of the resources at the back of the book.

When people talk about their money worries, they're invariably also worried about their status. 'If I have little money and no career, I'll have no status and end up being a dependent victim.' It would be more useful, I suggest, asking yourself what you're really afraid of:

- Not being able to afford the basics and to eat properly?

- Not being able to do the things I enjoy?

- Looking as though I've failed in the eyes of others and especially my children?

- Being without a job?

Having identified your concerns, you can now begin to look at how to manage. You mentioned that you had a lot to offer which is a wealth in itself. If your principal concern is about not having enough money for the basics, then you need to consider finding a supplementary job for as many hours as you need. An alternative is working for yourself. You never have to retire from that unless you want to and you'll be able to draw your pension at the same time. If that appeals, do the following exercise.

EXERCISE: SKILLS AUDIT

1. Write a list of all the things you can do – anything at all, in or out of work, big or small. You should have at least fifty things on this list.

2. Tick those things you enjoy doing.

3. What, from that list, could you do from home which could bring in an income? (Rachel's Dairy, the organic dairy products company, started as a simple idea in someone's kitchen! So have many clothes and travel companies.)

4. Do you know anyone with whom you could collaborate? Or do you have an idea that could involve your children? Maybe going into a joint business would be a way to let them help you financially. They could put in some initial capital and you could do the work.

A lot has been written on what makes a successful entrepreneur. (See Bibliography.) If you think this might suit you and you have an idea you'd like to pursue, take a look at the following questions.

EXERCISE: AM I AN ENTREPRENEUR AT HEART?

1. Am I really keen on my business idea?

2. Do I know enough about this subject to do it well? If not, move on to a new idea.

3. Is there someone already doing it for a price at which I couldn't compete?

4. What capital do I need to start this up? And where could I get it from? There are lots of government

bodies that can offer you advice and sometimes financial support.

5. What's my ambition – to cover the shortfall or make more money?

6. What do the consumers think? Try out your idea on other people and check if it will appeal.

If just thinking about developing your own enterprise gives you a buzz, you lose nothing if you put some energy into planning. It'll give you a focus which is both forward-thinking and creative, much more useful than worrying about lack of money. If your financial concerns are to do with less social standing, what could be better than having your own business, even if it doesn't make you a millionaire?

Q3 **I'm finding myself becoming obsessed with money. I'm 58 and, by being careful, I've just about had enough money to live on during the last few years. But I know I haven't put enough money into a pension. I never had any spare. How can I stop my anxiety keeping me awake at night and taking over my life?**

This concern about money has been discussed in the previous question. It's a common anxiety, but that doesn't make it any easier to bear or manage. We seem to be split into a number of groups: those who have worked for either the public sector or an organisation with a good pension deal, those who worked in smaller organisations whose scheme wasn't so good, those who decided to opt out of the pension scheme and those who were self-employed. Women often choose to pay the married woman's stamp which means that, unless you've paid in any extra, you'll get less of the already small state pension when you retire. Those who've been divorced may also find themselves in a vulnerable position.

Section 6, Question 5 would be good to explore. For now, I'm going to answer you with some different ideas that stem from the Emotional Freedom Technique (EFT) which is explained in Section 2, Question 3.

Before I go any further, I want to mention Carol Look, an EFT master, who has done a lot of work in the field of 'abundance'. Her book, *Attracting Abundance with EFT*, will give you numerous other ideas as will her website www.abundance.com. There are other sources of information in the Resource List. I will also introduce you to one of the ideas of Steve Wells and Dr David Lake who have developed Simple Energy Techniques and Provocative Energy Techniques; details can be found at www.eftdownunder.com. All their work, as explained earlier, stems from the techniques developed by Gary Craig.

No one could be a greater advocate than me of the benefits of talking and sharing views. But I also believe that other elements, such as our senses and our unconscious mind, shouldn't be over-looked. Very often we say one thing and do another. For example, you come in from work tired after a difficult day. You say to yourself, 'I won't watch any TV tonight. I'll have dinner, do what I need to do and go to bed.' Come 10.30 p.m. when every-thing is done, you go as if by magic to the TV and sit watching a film till 12.30 a.m. You can hardly keep your eyes open to the end. As you go to bed, you say to yourself, 'I don't know what I was doing watching that, I was so tired.' We use the self-same sabotage strategies in lots of situations and in your case I expect that applies when you're looking at ways to manage your income.

I explained the tapping sequence in Section 2, Question 3. If you haven't read that, or have forgotten it, I suggest you take a look now. Steve Wells and David Lake have modified the tapping sequence. The addition which I think would be helpful to try is the continual tapping of your fingers.

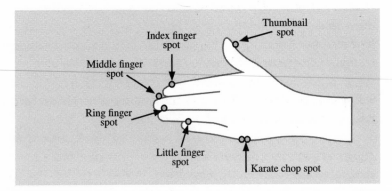

To do this, hold one hand out in front of you as in the diagram. The idea is to tap seven times on each of the finger points. Start by crossing your index finger over your thumb and tap on the side of your thumb. Then tap seven times on the outside side of each of your fingers using your thumb. Start with your index finger, now middle, then ring and then little finger and now return to the thumb and do it all over again. Repeat as many times as you can.

You can do this with both hands at once or just one. If you do the exercise for between half-an-hour and an hour a day for a month, I can pretty well guarantee that you'll feel better in yourself. Your energy will be moving through your system with fewer blips. Of course, I can't guarantee that you'll never have an off day but focusing on shifting the energy can only be good for you. I tap like this when I'm feeling stressed and, even though you don't have to think specifically about what's bothering you when you're doing it, it still often helps. If you put your hand in your pocket or behind your back, no one knows what you're doing! It's great for traffic jams or before any event that you're not looking forward to.

Carol Look in *Attracting Abundance with EFT* talks about the power of vibration. The theory states that everything vibrates and that, by increasing our positive vibrations, we can draw what we want towards us. The laws of attraction are written about by many and have recently been extolled in *The Secret*, a film produced by Prime Time Productions. It consists of a series of interviews and dramatisations related to the laws of attraction. It suggests people's feelings and thoughts attract real events in the world into their lives. There has been much controversy about this – but it's worth a look.

The principle is similar to many of my answers: by putting out a positive message and going for it, you're more likely to achieve your goals. The explanation of the law of attraction on www.abraham-hicks.com is clear and informative for those of you who want to know more. As with all these ideas, if they hit the right spot and feel right for you, then go for it. If it doesn't, then move on to something else that does, but don't fall into what can become a habit: dismissing an idea because it's new, not because you find by trying it out that it doesn't work.

I've found over the years that, although no idea has seemed to me to be the answer to all my problems, combining bits from a number of ideas has helped me sort out a variety of issues in my life. This doesn't, of course, mean that I no longer have issues; people who talk like that have their heads in the clouds. But what it does mean is that there are lots of techniques that oil the wheels as we travel along the tracks of life.

EXERCISE: MANAGING THOSE MONEY FEELINGS

Let's move now to a bit of practice. In your question you say, 'I know I haven't put enough money into a pension. I never had any spare.' The issue of not having enough is a good one for you to tap on. Think about the statement and number it 0–10, 10 being a high intensity of feeling and 0 being none.

Step 1: Tap the karate chop point and say, 'Even though I'm convinced there won't be enough for me and I'm attached to this belief, I deeply and completely love and accept myself anyway.' Do this three times.

Step 2: Say the negative phrases while tapping the sequence of eight points – eyebrow, side of eye, under eye, under nose, chin, collarbone, under arm, top of head.

Eyebrow: I've never had enough
Side of eye: There's never enough for me
Under eye: It'll probably be like this for ever
Under nose: I'll be short of money
Chin: It'll never change
Collarbone: Not enough is my lot
Under arm: I resent those who have it
Top of head: I'll never have enough

Step 3: Repeat these positive phrases while tapping the sequence of points.

Eyebrow: There is enough now and there will be enough later
Side of eye: I enjoy feeling satisfied
Under eye: I like knowing there's enough for me and others
Under nose: There's plenty for all
Chin: I can make enough for me
Collarbone: There will be enough for my future
Under arm: I feel satisfied with the money in my life
Top of head: I love knowing there is enough for me

Now take a deep breath and re-focus on the issue. Has it reduced from a 10 to a 6? If it's gone, move on to the next exercise: if not, tap on that issue a bit more. When you tap the negative phrases in further rounds add a 'still' or a 'little', whichever feels more appropriate, e.g. I still resent those who have money.

EXERCISE: FEELING SAFE AROUND MY FINANCES

This next exercise focuses on your fear of feeling unsafe:

Step 1: Tap on the karate chop point saying, 'Even though I'm really scared of being poor, and I'm convinced it has to be a struggle, I believe in myself and my ability to change my beliefs.' Do this three times.

Step 2: Say the negative phrases while tapping the sequence of eight points – eyebrow, side of eye, under eye, under nose, chin, collarbone, under arm, top of head.

Eyebrow: I've always found it hard to make ends meet
Side of eye: I never have enough to save
Under eye: I'm afraid to expect anything different
Under nose: I'm always short of money
Chin: I'm so scared of being poor
Collarbone: I don't know how to make it easy
Under arm: I've always struggled with money in my life
Top of head: Life and money-making are hard

Step 3: Repeat these positive phrases while tapping the sequence of points:

Eyebrow: I choose to change my beliefs
Side of eye: My fear is in the past
Under eye: I enjoy feeling free

Under nose: I believe I can have money
Chin: I plan to relax about money
Collarbone: I've found a new belief
Under arm: I'm free of my money fear
Top of head: I choose to enjoy the money I have

Now take a deep breath and re-focus on the issue. Has it reduced from a 10 to a 0? If it's gone, move on to the next exercise; if not, tap on that a little bit more but, when you tap the negative phrases, add a 'still' or a 'little', whichever feels more appropriate.

And now one for obsessional anxiety.

EXERCISE: MANAGING MY MONEY ANXIETY

Step 1: Tap the karate chop point and say three times, 'Even though I'm obsessed with my lack of money, and I believe I should worry about money, I deeply and completely accept who I am and my feelings.'

Step 2: Say the negative phrases while tapping the sequence of eight points – end of eyebrow, side of eye, under eye, under nose, chin, collarbone, under arm, top of head:

Eyebrow: I worry about money
Side of eye: I'm scared of having no money
Under eye: I can think about nothing but my lack of money
Under nose: I feel bad about not having enough money
Chin: I must be doing something wrong
Collarbone: I hate not having enough
Under arm: I will never have enough
Top of head: I worry about having no money

Step 3:

Eyebrow: I am free from my money worries
Side of eye: I love having money
Under eye: There's enough money for us all
Under nose: I enjoy having enough money
Chin: I feel good about the money I have
Collarbone: I'm relaxed about money
Under arm: I enjoy sharing my money
Top of head: I have enough money for my needs

Again, take a deep breath and tap further on it adding 'still' or 'a little' until the intensity of the feeling has reduced from a 10 to 2. You don't want it higher than that because it will go on doing for you what it has done so far and rooted you to the spot, unable to do anything to improve the situation. If it goes below a 2, you can become too laid back and therefore not do what is needing to be done.

I understand that your problem is real and feels really scary and needs some practical solutions. However, what I'm suggesting is that you take the fear out of it so your mind is free to come up with a solution. Alongside doing this, it's important that you get some practical help so you understand the figures and can make informed decisions. There are numerous financial advisors who can help you with money and pension advice. It's worth asking your friends if they can recommend someone or try talking to your bank. I've listed a few useful sources in the Resource List.

Q4 I've just turned 50 and I'm really fed up with my job. I want to leave but feel anxious about applying for anything new. How do I stop feeling trapped by my age?

You've turned 50 at the perfect time! Two factors are working in your favour. One is that new EU legislation came into force in October 2006 which outlaws discrimination on the basis of age. The other is that there will not be enough young people to fill all the job vacancies if all the early baby boomers take retirement. So they need you. It may have been true years ago that anyone over 50 was thought of as too old to learn and develop but it's a myth.

Having said that, it's not surprising that you have some concerns about changing jobs. We all know of people who've been made redundant and found it difficult to get a new job or the loyal worker who never gets promotion and there seems no reason for it except their age. This will become something of the past. Organisations are no longer able to ask on the application form for your date of birth or your whole educational and work history in a chronological order.

I appreciate that simply changing a law doesn't mean people's attitudes and values automatically change with it. I also know that, as I write this, cases are being prepared by lawyers and that, once age discrimination cases start to reach the courts, organisations take it all more seriously.

Another factor that affects a number of older workers (you may well be too young to be in this group) is that tertiary education was not common for all. Very few went to university: in the 1960s, 8 per cent of young people went to university; today, it's 40 per cent and rising. Many left school at 16 or 18 and went straight into a job, often secretarial. Many learnt at the side of the more experienced worker, a practice known colloquially as 'sitting by Nelly'. Some undertook vocational training and became nurses and teachers. Many expected to work until they had children, to take a break and then, if they went back at all, work part time.

All this changed as the baby boomer generation grew older. Today, young women expect to achieve at least as much as their male colleagues; they see their career as very important and not something that will be held back by having a family. Many 50+ women have far exceeded their original expectations.

Some, even if they're at the top of their tree, feel trapped in their job because they don't have on paper the qualifications that are often demanded by the job specification and therefore don't feel they can move. Further blocks are fears about losing their memory as they approach their sixties, and being slower at learning new skills, especially technological ones. Any permutation of these perceived problems can hold us back and whittle away our self-confidence.

I've explored the issue of self-confidence in Section 3, Question 1. Even though the questioner's concerns are different, the skills of developing self-confidence are the same, so please do those exercises first. I think you're being held back by what is called a limiting belief; in other words, something that you hold to be true – rightly or wrongly – and that affects how you think and behave.

I want to introduce you to a really useful theoretical idea called 'Logical Levels' which were created by Robert Dilts, one of the leading thinkers in the field of Neuro-Linguistic Programming. (See Bibliography.) If you take the sentence 'I CAN'T DO THIS HERE' and break it down into its individual words, you will see that they each have a specific meaning.

I – is my identity. It is who I am. It is my core self and values. Often, when you go to a party and meet someone new, one of the first things you're asked is, what do you do? How do you normally answer? Listen next time you ask someone. Some answer: 'I work at . . . ;' others say, 'I'm a . . .' If they say the latter you know they're very identified with that job. They see it as part of themselves – for example, 'I'm a doctor.' It is often people like this who can become depressed when they retire as they feel they've lost some of their identity.

CAN'T – is a belief. I often hear people say, 'It's impossible but I'll try.' They invariably fail! If you truly believe it's impossible, why try? If what you mean is, 'It may be difficult,' then that's a different story. Our beliefs affect what we do and our behaviour. A salesman who doesn't believe in his product can't sell it. A woman who doesn't believe in herself or her skills can't sell herself and get a new job.

DO – is a skill. You need skills to do an activity, for example, planning, baking or singing. If you don't know what you need to do in order to bake a cake or hit top C, you won't be able to do it. Often, when people don't manage to achieve something, it's not because they don't want to but because they don't have the necessary skills.

THIS – is the behaviour. You need to do a number of different behaviours/actions to undertake an activity successfully, for example, you need to do certain movements to swim, or drive.

HERE – this relates to the environment, context, time and place. I can't do this activity here because it isn't appropriate, for example, drinking a glass of wine in the office on an ordinary Monday morning, something I could do after work in the pub.

As you can see from the above, our beliefs are the cornerstones on which we base our thinking and behaviour. So, going back to your question, if you convince yourself you're too old, you'll act as though it's true, a self-fulfilling prophecy that will fool people into believing you really are a woman with no vitality, energy or anything to offer.

I'll let you into a secret: play make-believe and act as though it's real. It's amazing how many times others believe our performance and how quickly we find that it's become true. We've all held beliefs that we've long since abandoned – for example, at one stage in your life, you believed there was a Father Christmas who came down the chimney with the presents! Beliefs can change.

Nor are they 'givens' that we were born with. They're created through our experiences and upbringing. We build personal beliefs by generalising from our experience of the world and from others. Many of our beliefs about ourselves come from things said to us when we were young – for example, 'You're a very clever girl,' a good one to hold on to. 'You aren't as clever as your sister,' on the other hand, is one to be dumped. Positive beliefs empower and encourage us. Learning is fun, for instance, is so much more helpful than a limiting negative belief that learning is hard.

The following exercise will help you to create good positive beliefs so you can tackle any situation with the belief you can do it.

EXERCISE: CREATING POSITIVE BELIEFS

1. Write down five beliefs that you hold that are positive – for example, 'I've got a nice face.'

2. Write down five limiting beliefs – for example, 'I'm not very good at learning languages.'

3. Now write down what you've missed in your life because of these – for example, taking up a holiday job in Italy because you were worried about the language. (This may not feel comfortable but, by identifying the effect these negative beliefs have had on you, it will encourage you to drop them.)

4. Now write down five beliefs that you would like to have – for example, 'I can learn anything I want.'

5. Now, in order to really believe this, you need to reinforce this new message to create a new thinking habit. (See Section 6, Question 2.) One of the ways to do this is to create affirmations – for example, 'I'm a good learner.' Make a positive affirmation for each of your new positive beliefs.

6. Make a commitment to yourself to repeat these daily, six times a day, starting with when you wake up and ending with when you go to sleep.

Once you believe in yourself and know that you can get any job you want, there'll be no stopping you – and I bet no one even notices your age!

Q5 **I know I need a new challenge. I've talked with my friends and some say I'm mad to want to change careers at 55 although others have been encouraging. I'm uncertain what I have to offer a new job, what I want to do, or how to go about it. I've been sitting on the fence far too long. How do I get off?**

It sounds as though you've been doing what you've been doing for quite a while and that your job-seeking skills need a polish. I talk about change in the next question. Please take a look at that to help you understand how you approach change and why others see it differently. I'm going to focus my answer on how you find a new job/career.

When we reach 50+, we can get caught up with concerns about our age which block us from getting what we want. I know a woman who came back to live in the UK after 25 years abroad. She had run her own small business which had recently folded. She believed that, if she had stayed in the UK, she would have been at the top of her profession. She couldn't see why that would be different now.

When she saw a very prestigious vacancy, she decided to apply. Most of her friends tried to put her off but she wasn't having it. She knew that she no longer understood the system as so many new regulations had come into place. Instead of letting this daunt her, she went to a coach and learnt the necessary skills. She's now employed in a very high-powered job. We can let our fears run us or we can harness that energy and make them work for us.

What you have to offer is unique – nobody else will do it like you. We often forget this and therefore offer a rather bland version of ourselves which works against potential success.

Below is a three-stage plan. Follow this and that dream job could be yours.

EXERCISE: PLANNING A NEW CAREER

Stage 1

1. What are your skills and talents? Write down all the skills you have. Even if you think they're unimportant or so simple that everyone has them. Gather these skills from all parts of your life – home, social and work. If you can follow a recipe, you can follow instructions. If you find you always add a variation, you're creative! What are the skills you used to have and have forgotten about, like organising a sponsored charity walk when you were at school or your children's school fair? What do you do socially? What are the things you do that make others say, 'I couldn't do that'? It could be baking bread before you go to work or discussing something difficult with your child's headmistress. And remember the basics like reading, writing and arithmetic!

2. Now you've got your skills list, divide it into basic, special and personality skills – for example, honest, trustworthy and logical. If you're stuck on this one, think about how others would describe you. You can always ask them. I was at a wedding a while back and the 'best woman' gave the bride a small silk book with all her qualities written down in it. One word to a page. The recipient was more thrilled with this than any other present and has cherished it ever since.

3. So you now know what you're capable of, although that doesn't mean it's what you like doing – tidying drawers and clearing clutter, for instance. What are the things that give you a buzz? Think of five occasions when you've had a really good time. What was it that made it so good? Write down all the factors. Are there any patterns? Don't worry if some seem to conflict with each other. As you think of these scenarios, if any as yet unlisted skills and talents pop up that aren't on your previous list, just add them now.

4. Now organise your skills and talents into clusters. The best way to do this is to take your skills and look at what you can do with them – for example, problem-solve, teach, manage people (remember not everything has to come from your working life).

Stage 2

1. You know your abilities and qualities so you know exactly what you can offer and at what level. But where do you want to do it? Your first task is to put your attributes into priority order. Which are the most important to you? For example, organised. Decide if this an attribute you want to use at work and in which way. If you enjoy organising things, then you need a role where you can

use this skill, e.g. office manager. If, however, you can 'do' organised but it bores you, then you may need to look for a job where you can be more creative, for instance, setting up a design studio. If you're stuck, remind yourself of the times you've enjoyed. What made the events so enjoyable? List those attributes at the top. Also think about the things you don't like in your job or in other parts of your life. You want to find a job with as few of these as possible. (The exercise in Section 3, Question 5 on values would be helpful to do here.)

2. If you want to move into a new field of work, you'll need to show that you have the relevant competence to undertake the tasks you'll have to tackle and evidence to prove your capabilities. Preparation is the key so take your skills and think of examples where you've used them and what you achieved. The more familiar you are with these examples, the easier it will be for you to talk about them when asked.

Stage 3

1. Next, you need to identify what you want to do. Because of particular circumstances in our lives, we often bury our desires. One way to overcome this is to daydream, allowing yourself to remember early dreams right from when you were a child. You may be surprised by forgotten desires that pop into your mind. Hold on to them this time. This is your opportunity to pursue them. (See Section 1, Question 1.)

2. Make a list of your interests – fishing, baking, fashion, animals and so on. With others, brainstorm all the possible careers where these interests could be pursued. Now cross off the ones that don't interest you – it may be zookeeper, or those that need a qualification you

haven't got or don't want to pursue. If you like helping people but hate hospitals being a nurse is clearly a non-starter. You should now have a list of possible new careers. While doing this, think (as they say) out of the box – in other words, think more broadly than you normally would. Don't restrict yourself, even if your ideas at present seem a bit implausible. The timeline exercise in Section 1, Question 1 is a good one to help you make sure you're going to achieve all you want, and look at problem-solving in Section 1, Question 5.

Stage 4

1. The next and final stage is now to go and get the ideal job that uses your skills and meets your desires. You've probably got a lot of possible avenues in front of you which need to be prioritised. Some may be areas you know little about so do some research. Make an appointment to talk to someone in that field. Find out everything you can so you can make an informed choice. Ask if you can do a day's work shadowing (older people can do that, too!). Many organisations are delighted that someone is interested enough to want to come to visit. We are all flattered when people are interested in what we are doing. Make sure they know you're just looking. It's very important that it's not linked to a post they've advertised. Or you could call someone in the field for a chat and ask to pick their brains. Being consulted as an expert is something we all love!

2. Having gathered all the information, you're ready to decide where you want to focus your attention and what kind of post you want to apply for.

Armed with all this knowledge about yourself, your skills and the post, you'll be very desirable to any employer. If you couple this with enthusiasm (easy when you've chosen your career), there'll be no stopping you.

Q6 **My husband and I are coming up to retirement – all a bit daunting! I've never been good with change. I'm not sure what I'm going to do with my time. I think I should probably travel. I know that unless I go soon I'll miss out. My husband seems to be approaching retirement so differently. He positively relishes the prospect of change.**

The ways we respond to change will be a pattern we've developed over the years. There's a model for looking at change devised by Rupert Eales White that bases itself on the Herrmann thinking preferences. (See Question 1 of this section.) If we understand our patterns of behaviour, we have much more hope of managing them rather than them managing us. It also helps us understand others around us who may do things differently.

You say that the idea of this imminent change in your life is worrying you and obviously causing you some stress. What happens to all of us when stressed is that we revert to our preferred way of behaving, dig in and find it hard to take any advice or to engage positively with the change process. You quite clearly aren't yet there, otherwise you wouldn't be asking for advice. The following questionnaire should help you to take change in your stride.

EXERCISE: MY CHANGE PREFERENCE STYLE

I. Answer all the questions. In each category, there are four choices; choose the word with which you identify most. Give your first choice 4 marks, 3 marks to your next choice, then 2 and finally 1 mark for the one with which you least identify.

1. Jobs	Marks	
Researcher	A	
Administrator	B	
Writer	C	
Social worker	D	

2. Words	Marks	
Harmony	A	
Beauty	B	
Intellect	C	
Efficiency	D	

3. Words	Marks	
Keep	A	
Evaluate	B	
Share	C	
Change	D	

4. Words	Marks	
Idea	A	
Feeling	B	
Organisation	C	
Fact	D	

5. Phrases	Marks	
The right answer	A	
Safety first	B	
Go for it	C	
Sixth sense	D	

6. Sayings	Marks	
Smile and the whole world smiles with you	A	
Nothing ventured, nothing gained	B	
The facts speak for themselves	C	
Look before you leap	D	

7. How someone who did not like you might describe you	Marks	
Being stuck in the mud	A	
Being as dry as dust	B	
Wearing your heart on your sleeve	C	
Having your head in the clouds	D	

8. Attitude to risk. Do you prefer to:	Marks	
Take risks	A	
Share risks	B	
Avoid risks	C	
Analyse risks	D	

9. Attitude to change. Do you prefer to:	Marks	
Analyse and evaluate ideas	A	
Implement ideas that are practical	B	
Generate ideas	C	
Look to see how ideas will affect others	D	

10. Actions you take. Do you prefer to:	Marks	
Make a new friend	A	
Change your approach	B	
Have a debate	C	
Control a situation	D	

11. How you would describe yourself	Marks	
Practical	A	
Rational	B	
Friendly	C	
Imaginative	D	

12. How might someone who didn't like you describe you	Marks	
Rebellious	A	
Weak	B	
Over-cautious	C	
Cold	D	

2. Score yourself on the scoring sheet below. Transfer each mark into the appropriate column. When you've completed the form, add up your totals and fill in the scorecard.

Scoring

Question								
No.	LD		CC		PF		PC	
1.	A		B		D		C	
2.	C		D		A		B	
3.	B		A		C		D	
4.	D		C		B		A	
5.	A		B		D		C	
6.	C		D		A		B	
7.	B		A		C		D	
8.	D		C		B		A	
9.	A		B		D		C	
10.	C		D		A		B	
11.	B		A		C		D	
12.	D		C		B		A	
Sub-totals			+		+		+	
					TOTAL	=	120	

Your Profile

Preference	LD	CC	PF	PC
	50			
	48			
	46			
High	44			
	42			
	40			
	38			
	36			
	34			
Medium	32			
	30			
	28			
	26			
	24			
	22			
	20			
	18			
	16			
	14			
	12			
SCORE				

Example

Preference	LD	CC	PF	PC
	50			
	48			
	46			
High	44			
	42			
	40			
	38			
	36			
	34			
Medium	32			
	30			
	28			
	26			
	24			
	22			
	20			
	18			
	16			
	14			
	12			
SCORE	22	28	40	34

3. Plot your score on the graph above so you can see it visually in relation to the other columns.

4. Ned Herrmann's divisions of the brain are explained below:

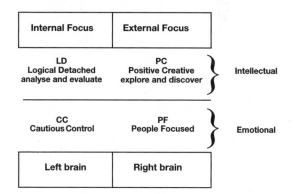

Internal Focus	External Focus	
LD Logical Detached analyse and evaluate	**PC** Positive Creative explore and discover	} Intellectual
CC Cautious Control	**PF** People Focused	} Emotional
Left brain	Right brain	

5. So which one are you? Read the following for the description of each type.

Remember – none of us stay in just one quadrant all of the time but we do in the main have a preferred style which we take refuge in when stressed or scared.

The **Logical Detached** person has an unemotional and rational perspective to any change. They're interested in the facts of the matter and the implications. They're unlikely to challenge the nature and dimension of the change or consider the emotional impact on themselves or others but will focus on analysing the situation. The positive side is that they're careful, meticulous, logical and analytical; they'll have worked out their finances and analysed what's available for them when they retire. They'll be eager to ensure that every step continues to be analysed, evaluated and modified if there's any deviation.

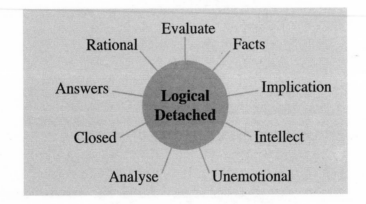

The **Cautious Control** person wants to keep the status quo and is particularly interested in how the change will affect them, and those they identify with. Their general stance is negative and they're willing to express their views with any argument that comes into their mind. At times, they can appear to others to be illogical and emotional. A person acting from this position does not see themselves like this, which in itself can cause difficulty in communication. On the positive side, their resistance to change means they're cautious and often able to help other, more impetuous, people to reconsider before making mistakes. Once they're either convinced of the advantages of the change or realise that the change is going to happen whatever they do, they use their organisational and practical skills to ensure that the change occurs in a planned, timely and efficient manner.

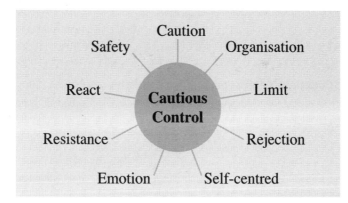

The **People Focused** person just accepts the change and doesn't appear to be fazed by it personally. Their reactions are generally emotional, both for themselves and their family. They show concern for others and help them to manage their situations. They involve others and share their experiences. The positive side of this is that they often help others to express their emotions so they can be understood. The downside is that they get stuck with their feelings – whether it be misery, happiness or anger – and find it difficult to see beyond this. If feelings are not discussed, they'll find other ways of expressing themselves and this can cause problems. Even more importantly, though, they often forget about themselves as they're so worried about others. They can often end up feeling resentful and taking the role of the victim.

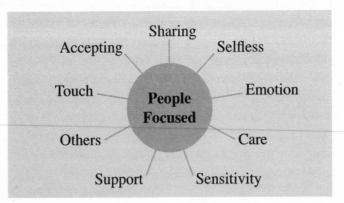

The **Positive Creative** person loves the idea of change. They get excited, want it to happen as soon as possible and look forward to the challenges that it brings. They always look on the bright side of life and are always stimulated by new viewpoints. They get their energy from taking risks and having new adventures. They don't focus on the emotional impact of the situation on themselves or others. When they have an idea, they can become single-minded and very pushy and demanding in order to meet their goals, with little tolerance of other views. On the positive side, they're very future-orientated, big-picture, imaginative thinkers who see multiple possibilities within any situation. They thrive on change rather than being scared by it.

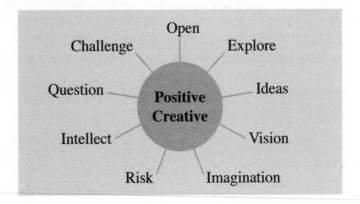

Doing the questionnaire and reading this, you will be able to identify where you are and where your husband is. The pairs that find it the most difficult to manage change together are those who are diagonally opposite each other in the chart. So, for example, the Cautious Control person believes the Positive Creative person, who thinks they should just down tools the day they finish working and get on a plane and go somewhere for three months, is irresponsible. The Positive Creative person thinks the Cautious Control person is always moaning, forever worried about everything and never exists in the moment.

The Logical Detached person knows they're right: they've done the sums and worked out where they can travel safely and within budget while leaving everything safe and in order at home. The fact the People Focused person is worried about their mother, the children, the neighbours and so on is enough to drive them mad. Whilst the People Focused person thinks the Logical Detached person doesn't really care about anyone but themselves and never probably really loved the children anyway!

So what to do? First, and most importantly, is to recognise that people behave as they do because they're worried; they just may show it differently. Then acknowledge their viewpoint – for example, tell your partner you know it would be exciting to get on a plane and head off into the wide blue yonder but that if you could do x or y first, you'd find it so much easier. If you validate the other person's point of view, they'll be much more willing to listen to you. Enjoy!

Q7 **I've always wanted to travel abroad and spend some time living somewhere else. I'm now getting to the age when, unless I do it soon, I'm not going to have the energy. I don't have close friends or family to travel with or much**

money. I'm wondering about taking a career break but I'm neither ready nor can I afford to retire. I've watched young people take, as their right, a gap year or two! I feel it's my turn. What opportunities are there for someone in her mid-fifties? And how will this affect my life back home?

I am sure you, like me, remember when people left school and either went straight into a job or on to higher education and then into a job. It was unusual to have time off. Now, as you so rightly say, young people believe that a gap year is a right of passage to adulthood. Colleges encourage it and even those who choose to go straight to work often find a way to have a break first. Let's hope that, in time, career breaks for the older person will be as commonplace as gap years for the young. It looks like it's already started. A survey undertaken by American Express found that more than a third of all gap-year travellers were people aged over 55. A 2005 Mintel report, *Gap Year Travel*, estimated that 520,000 Britons take a gap-year trip abroad each year, of whom 90,000 are on career breaks and 200,000 are 55 and over.

You sound as though you think there's an upper age limit to travelling but that just isn't the case so don't feel that, if you don't go this year, you'll have missed out for ever. Many take a period of time away when they retire. However, you say that what you think you want is a career break, with the chance to come back again, so the time sounds ripe right now. As you're unsure, try the career break quiz below to help you make up your mind.

EXERCISE: CAREER BREAK QUIZ

1. How long have you been in employment or running your own business?

   a)   A few months

   b)   Fifteen years plus

   c)   Ten to fifteen years

   d)   Under five years

2. How stressed do you feel?

   a)   Cool and calm

   b)   Tearing your hair out

   c)   Depends on the day but more than less

   d)   Occasionally

3. How often do you spend time helping others, either informally or as a volunteer?

   a)   I only have time for myself

   b)   Often – I like being with people and helping

   c)   I do and then get exhausted and stressed by it

   d)   I try to but run out of time

4. How often do you start the week wishing it were Friday?

   a)   Only if I've had a heavy weekend – work's fine

   b)   I dread Mondays

c) Whenever we have a deadline to meet

d) Occasionally when my colleagues are on holiday

5. Do you like to travel and want to see the world?

a) I've done a lot already

b) I'm longing to see what's out there and how others live

c) I've seen a lot of Europe

d) I've done some travelling but would like to see more at some point

6. If you were given six months' salary would you:

a) Give up work for six months and hang out

b) Go and see the world

c) Pay it into a pension fund

d) Do your house up

Scoring: score 1 for every a) answer, 2 for every d), 3 for every c) and 4 for every b). Now, add up your points.

1–6: you aren't ready to go, you sound settled and it's a good time to get on with your home life.

7–12: toy with the idea but don't put it top of your agenda. Work out what you want to do over the next five years and start planning.

13–18: This may be right for you. You're a bit uncertain at the moment and have a few issues to sort out first. Ask yourself, is fear holding you back?

19–24: Go for it! Do your planning and research and pack your bags.

A career break is different from a holiday and retirement. It's you actively deciding to stop working for a while and planning to go back to earning money at the end of the break. It gives you the opportunity to do something different while recharging your batteries which inevitably get a bit flat through the daily grind of modern life. The break can be for a couple of months; it doesn't need to be a year. As well as giving you the chance to de-stress and fill your memory banks with new experiences, it will also allow you to develop new skills.

Many people report on their return that they feel like a different person with a new outlook on life. Some find they want to start down a new career path or to begin a new business. If you've brought up a family and they've now left home, it'll give you the opportunity to be someone different and not be seen just as someone's mum! It's also an opportunity to meet new people from other walks of life and do something new. You might opt to do some volunteer work.

It's great to have old friends and those deep connections but also good to explore other types of relationships. Choosing to do it now, as you said, will give you a chance to do something challenging that you may feel less able to do when you're 80.

Don't think that career breaks are only for the single. Many couples choose to go together and some organisations positively welcome a self-sufficient pair, who may be happier to go somewhere remote, rather than a single person. Also, many couples are recognising that they have different goals and aspirations and that it's all right for one of them to travel, even if the other would rather stay at home. If things are negotiated and both parties are happy, a period pursuing your own desires often strengthens a relationship.

There are a few things you need to consider when thinking about a career break. First, find out from the Human Resource people in your organisation what the company policy and attitudes are to sabbaticals, paid and unpaid. Some firms see this as part of normal modern-day life and a way to encourage their older skilled workers to remain part of the workforce although they won't pay you while you're away; others will give you a period of paid leave.

Your absence will allow someone immediately below you to develop their skills so it represents good succession planning. More junior posts could be filled by a temp. Remember when negotiating that, if your company is meeting you halfway, you need to offer something back such as training up your temporary successor or taking your break at a time that suits the organisation. If they won't allow you a break on any terms and you feel strongly about it, then you'll have to consider resigning. Then you'll be free to start something new when you return. With the Age Discrimination Act now in place, there should be no problem getting a job at 55+.

Financing your break is important, and can be trickier than when you were 18 with few responsibilities. You also may not want to backpack this time round or sleep in a room with lots of others or, to put it another way, it's going to cost more! The amount of money you'll need will depend on what it is you plan to do. If you want to travel the world staying in five-star hotels, it'll obviously be extremely expensive. And, while there's nothing wrong with doing that, I'm guessing that wouldn't be your choice.

Some countries are going to be much cheaper to travel in than others. Travelling in India, for example, will be less than half the cost of travelling in Japan. The kind of break you want will depend entirely on you. Some people just want to relax, see new places and experience new cultures; others want to live in a community, give something back and become involved in voluntary projects. Then again, not everyone wants to go abroad for their 'gap year'. There are numerous places in the UK to explore, and many charities looking for volunteers.

There are a number of organisations set up for just for this; gap years for the over-fifties is a booming business. I've listed a few in the Resource List. As well as giving you lots of suggestions of where and what you can do, they also offer good advice.

You say you want to live somewhere else and your resources are limited. One of the best ways to do this is via volunteer work. Although many of the schemes will charge you something to cover the costs of the arrangements and your accommodation and food, it will amount to much less than staying in hotels. And it'll give you the opportunity to experience how people live in different cultures and a chance to give back to the world by helping people, working on the environment or offering your skills via teaching and educating. Health professionals, engineers and accountants are all in demand in developing countries and paid work is sometimes available. Whatever your skills, you'll be welcome. Many of the schemes also throw in tourist visits and weekend activities where you see sights you'd miss if you were travelling on your own.

If you're contemplating a volunteer break, it's often possible to raise some money through friends or at work and, if half the money goes directly to the project and half towards getting you there, most people are happy to contribute. To raise funds, you could set up a supper quiz, sell cakes, make lunch for your colleagues at work, do a sponsored run or silence or whatever appeals.

It's definitely worth planning your finances carefully so you know exactly how much you'll need to keep you while you're away. Make sure you'll be able to cover all your outgoings, which may well include maintaining your home in the UK. There are a number of internet sites that can help you, for example www.grownup-gapyear.co.uk and www.gapadvice.org. If you're going away for more than six months, you could rent out your home.

It's often helpful to talk to an accountant or financial advisor about all of these things, including whether you should continue paying into your pension scheme and how much tax you are due back. It's very helpful to have a little money waiting for you when you return. All this may sound a bit dull but it's essential if this break is going to be the chance of a lifetime you've dreamt about for so long.

In summary, do your planning, look up places on the internet, choose an organisation you want to travel with, ask 101 questions, speak to others who've done the same thing so you feel really confident in your decisions – and have the time of your life!

∽ Section Six ∾

You're Never Too Old to ... Feel Good

Many of us will have been brought up to believe that when we get to a certain age – and certainly well before we're 60 – we'll start to fall apart, our bodies will become prone to aches and pains, our agility hampered, and our minds losing their edge. Physically and mentally, it'll be downhill all the way!

And yet, nothing could be further from the truth. We're living longer with ample opportunity to develop our minds and keep our bodies in good shape. In many ways, baby boomers are pioneers. Most of us will have watched previous generations become more frail and less fit as they entered their sixties and seventies. Our greatest challenge is to find ways to do things differently: something we're already achieving.

But it can be bewildering. We're bombarded on an almost daily basis with information about how to be physically and mentally alert which, as the following questions illustrate, can send out mixed messages. I hope the answers will help separate the wheat from the chaff.

Q **I've just had my fiftieth birthday and, every time I read a newspaper or a magazine, articles jump out at me about all the health problems that can happen to the over-fifties. I've convinced myself that I will lose my memory, get Alzheimer's, have dementia, a weak bladder, a face like a prune, brown age-spots all over, get osteoporosis, lose interest in sex, put on weight around my middle – and all before I reach 60! What can I do and what do I need to eat to keep myself healthy and fit?**

Our generation has seen a real change in the amount of information available about health, fitness and diet. There is a sports club near almost everyone's home, while more swimming pools also offer gym facilities. Alternative therapists are now seen as mainstream and there are health-food shops in most high streets. We are all much more aware of our health than our parents were and certainly our grandparents.

Our own personal care and knowledge together with medical science mean that most of us will live longer than the previous generation. But that also means we're asking our bodies to work longer. Lifespan projections are changing. It's no longer 'three score years and ten'. On average, women still live longer than men but the gap is decreasing.

Figures from the Office for National Statistics show that, in recent years, 'the increase in life expectancy among older adults has been dramatic. (See statistics on page 134.) Those of us in our fifties are likely to live even longer. There's a good chance that a child born today will easily reach over a 100.

There is a wide variety of views on how to be healthy and live longer and no wonder: every day there are conflicting reports in the papers about what is good for us. There will always be exceptions to any rule but looking after yourself and making sure you're healthy and moderately fit clearly makes good sense. We all know people who've become obsessed with their health and obsession of any sort is never a good thing. Moderation in all things is what I would advocate.

It's also pretty clear to me that, if you're walking around wheezing and struggling to get out of your chair or finding it hard to run for the bus, you'll look older than someone who does everything easily. Obviously, if you have a particular health condition, you can't be blamed if you're not looking good for your age. But there's no excuse for never exercising or for eating too much. What kind of image do you want to project to the world?

I've discussed exercise in Question 4 of this section so I'm going to focus here on diet. There are lots of sources of information on diet. All you need to do is go to your local library or book-shop or Google 'health and fitness for the over-fifties' on the internet. If you're somewhat cynical about some of the advice, stick to the more recognised sites or organisations. (See the Resource List.)

I will outline briefly what to eat when you are starting out on changing your eating habits. Foods that are rich in starch and fibre are good for you. The starch is good, clean body fuel, giving you instant energy, while the fibre will help to prevent constipation and reduce the risk of intestinal disorders including bowel cancer. Iron-rich foods help keep up your body's store of iron, particularly important if you're suffering from heavy periods. It's a good idea to avoid drinking tea or coffee with iron-rich food as this can affect how much iron the body absorbs. Foods and drinks rich in vitamin C are thought to help the body absorb iron. Foods containing folic acid help maintain good health in older age, reducing the risk of heart disease, cervical abnormalities, cancer and diabetes mellitus. Calcium-rich foods are essential for bones. Osteoporosis is a major health concern for older people, particularly women. This is where bone density reduces and so the risk of fractures increases.

Weight is also an issue. As you grow older, being overweight will affect your mobility which, in turn, can affect your health and your quality of life. It can also make you prey to heart disease and diabetes. Sudden weight loss can be cause for concern, too. It may mean that either you're not eating enough food or that you're not 100 per cent well. So check it out.

If you want to know whether you're the right weight for your age and height, you can use a number of different methods. The Body Mass Index (BMI) measures the ratio of your weight to your height. The formula to work this out is your weight (in kilograms) divided by your height (in metres) squared. Your BMI should be between 20 and 25. If the figure is higher than this, you are considered overweight.

Another good barometer is waist-to-hip ratio. You can work out your waist-to-hip ratio by dividing the measurement of your waist by that of your hips. For men, a ratio should ideally not be over 0.9. For women, the figure is 0.85. The higher the number above these values, the greater your risk of heart disease.

If you have too much weight around your middle, this increases your risk of developing heart disease and diabetes. If the weight is around your hips – the classic 'pear' shape – you're probably doing all right. Someone with an apple shape will face greater health risks than someone who has a pear shape, even if they're both overweight. Use the Ashwell® shape chart to see whether you are a chilli, apple, apple/pear or pear. (See www.eatwell.gov.uk.)

You should be able to get vitamins and minerals from your food. Like calcium, vitamin D is important for good bone health. We absorb it from sunshine, but go easy: too much sun can be harmful. You should aim to keep your salt intake low because it can cause high blood pressure, but make sure you eat enough potassium (found in bananas, dried apricots and fish). Regular moderate alcohol may decrease heart-attack risk although drinking heavily can damage the liver and can also adversely affect blood pressure.

Make sure you eat lots of fruit and veg, as they're full of anti-oxidants, which are essential in healthy cell regeneration; the more we consume, the better our cells will replicate. You should eat up to ten portions a day as you get older. It's also a good idea to reduce calorie intake, which will help to increase longevity. Drinking lots of water is also important – eight glasses (1.2 litres) every day will guard against getting dehydrated.

Fish is better for you than red meat as it's an excellent source of protein and contains many vitamins and minerals. Saturated fats and sugars need to be eaten in moderation: having too much fat can increase the amount of cholesterol in the blood, a trigger for heart disease. Sugary foods and drinks can also cause tooth decay. Teeth are certainly good examples of how looking after them makes a difference. The percentage of adults with their own teeth bears no resemblance to the figures even 30 years ago. Figures for adults with 20 or more of their own teeth have risen from 73 per cent in 1978 to 80 per cent in 1988 to 83 per cent 10 years later. The largest improvement is in the 65–75 age group – almost half have their own teeth compared to only a quarter 10 years previously. Foods that contain added sugar are also often high in calories, again not great for the waistline.

In the Bibliography, you'll find a list of books and websites with a wealth of information. Go well!

Q2 We're told that a positive mind equals positive health. That's all well and good. The problem is, I don't know what that really means and I certainly don't know how to achieve it. As I grow older, my greatest goal is to remain healthy. What do you advise?

Negative thinking is common to many of us. We all do it sometimes. For some, it's a habit learnt as a child; others have a predisposition to feeling down or anxious or angry. Negative thinkers tend to use language that promotes negativity. The language we use has an effect on our emotions and our behaviour. 'I'll never achieve anything at work' or 'I'll never meet a new partner' can become self-fulfilling prophecies, encouraging the person to give up before they've started. If you find yourself using words like 'ought to' and 'must', it may be an indication that you're becoming judgemental or critical. All of this can lead to a person feeling down. Do you recognise any of this?

Positive minds, on the other hand, do indeed lead to more positive health. Positive thinking helps us to be creative and forward thinking. It improves our immune system so it works more efficiently and therefore helps heal our bodies more quickly and effectively.

There are some who say we should be positive all the time but I'd caution a little perspective. We all have bad times; occasions when it's appropriate to be cross or sad. I remember a client saying to me once that she wanted to be happy all the time. I queried 'all the time' and she said, 'I mean always.' I then asked her if she wanted to be happy at her mother's funeral. 'Don't be crazy,' she said, 'of course not.' It's important to be clear when it's appropriate to think positively and when not.

Feelings and moods are an essential ingredient of what makes us tick. Problems arise, though, if we get taken over by our emotions, if they start controlling us rather than the other way around. I wonder how negative you really are. Scientists studying moods have found that we register our negative moods much more than our positive ones and therefore these are the moods we focus on, remember and replay. (See Section 1, Question 3 for more on association.) Try this exercise.

EXERCISE: THINKING IT THROUGH

1. Get hold of a stopwatch and set it to beep every hour. Do it for a few hours at a time and over several days, varying the time of day.

2. Note down your mood each time you hear a beep. You'll be self-conscious to begin with but very soon afterwards you'll forget to manufacture your moods for the stopwatch.

3. Do this for two or three days, including at least one weekend day.

4. Now analyse your notes – for what percentage of the day do you feel negative? What are the causes? These negative thoughts will give you a clue about what needs to change.

Where we often go wrong is in focusing on the mood and its cause rather than on how we'd like to be instead and how to change things. So, for example, your partner has just done something that upsets you. You can sulk or shout or cry. Or you can note there's a problem and talk to them about how to deal with it. Even if you decide not to talk it through, you can decide for yourself what you'd like to do and that can include thinking about something else rather than letting the mood swallow you up.

If thinking like this isn't your style and you want to change, you'll have to decide to do it consciously and then work at it. One way to practise learning to control your emotions is to write down your feelings as they happen. It's a good way to get them out of your system and in a place where you can come back to when you're less overwhelmed and can work out how to manage the situation.

One trick for changing your mood fast is to smile; ideally at something you find funny although even a false one helps. It tells your brain you're feeling fine and the happy hormone, serotonin, is produced, instantly making you feel better. Why not 'create' a file in your brain containing particular jokes or pictures that make you smile? One woman I worked with who'd become a slave to her sulkiness remembered a joke her father had told when she was young. Whenever she felt bad, she told herself this joke and then laughed at the memory of her and her sister having to leave the table before they wet themselves. It immediately made her feel better.

Positive thinkers, even when things are going badly and they have a right to be cross or disappointed, are very quick to find a way to harness hope. Hope gives us the feeling that things will happen to make it a better future. This gives us energy and really can enhance our health. People who have hope are more likely to succeed in anything they attempt at home, work or play.

Hope gives us the necessary boost to keep persevering at a task and solving the problem. It's important to believe better things are possible. Positive people tend to focus on more than one goal. If something doesn't work out the way they want, they turn to something else to minimise the disappointment. The phrase 'Don't put all your eggs in one basket' is useful to remember.

Here's a good regime to follow to help you manage your feelings:

1. Recognise the negative emotions going on inside you. Are you sad/angry/resentful/jealous?

2. Name them and acknowledge you have them. Suppressing them takes a lot of energy and they'll pop out again, often at the most inopportune moment.

3. Try to pin down the cause. Is it aimed at the world, one person, a group?

4. Now decide what you're going to do about it. Can you get rid of this feeling by yourself? Do you need to talk to a friend about it or the person or people involved? Choose your course of action.

5. If you're really stuck, go and talk to a professional who can help. This is particularly useful if you know you've been experiencing these feelings for a while.

Many of us in our fifties and older were brought up not to show emotion or ask for help. But expressing your feelings is essential if you're going to release the negative within. It's important to realise that you can manage your emotions and you can choose your emotional state. This will give you choices you may not have realised you had.

EXERCISE: THINK BEAUTIFUL

Find a quiet place to sit. Then think about a situation you're not looking forward to. Consider the following questions:

1. How would I prefer to think and feel?

2. When did I last feel good?

3. Remember and visualise this experience. I can choose to feel like that now.

4. Create new thoughts, breathe evenly and relax your muscles, especially your shoulders and around the mouth, and stand or sit in the way you would when feeling confident and good.

5. Create a mental video and imagine yourself feeling good.

6. Be in the moment: focus on what is happening now.

7. Now run the future scenario through and note how much easier it feels.

If you've got into the habit of negative thinking, you can forget how to be positive. The following exercise will help you to hold on to a positive emotion.

EXERCISE: THINK POSITIVE

1. Think of a time when you had a positive state of mind. This can be at any time of your life and in any situation.

2. Identify what thoughts, sounds, emotional and physical feelings you experienced when in a positive state of mind.

3. Say them out loud and see what it does for you.

4. Note that the state of being positive does not have to depend upon a particular situation but can be conjured up through memory and imagination at any time or place in your life.

5. Now stand up and imagine that you're back in the positive situation you thought of in 'Think Beautiful'. Remember the situation as if you were in it today. Relive all aspects of the internal experience of being positive. Fully associate with the event.

6. Identify a word that will remind you of this positive state so you can focus on feeling positive whenever you choose.

A final and really important point to remember is that emotions are infectious. How one person is feeling almost always impacts on those around them. If someone's depressed, it tends to bring other people down; if someone's angry, it can cause fear in others. One short explosion can irreparably change a relationship. If you feel good, others will feel good around you.

Q3 **I'm coming up to my sixtieth birthday and I'm dreading it! I felt like this on my fiftieth birthday and didn't have a good time although actually my fifties have been OK. The trouble is 60 feels so much older and a real start of being old. I'd like to look forward to it. How do I do that?**

Congratulations, you've made it! Well, almost . . . So why aren't we able to congratulate ourselves and bask in our achievements? Why do we find ourselves instead feeling sad and anxious that we have reached this age?

Women have always regarded 60 as a landmark. For a long time, it was the age at which we'd retire and therefore it's inextricably linked with being old. This is, of course, changing as working conditions for men and women are equalised. Women born in 1955 or after will have to wait until they're 65 to draw their state pension.

Until recently, most jobs had a retirement age around 60. But now there's much more choice. Even if your organisation has a retirement age, it will be 65 for both genders although more and more employers have done away with the concept of retirement entirely. We baby boomers are again being given a choice – much like when we were being offered the Pill. We've been able to choose when to have children and now whether to retire or not.

In my experience, those who have opted for self-employment rarely think about retiring in relation to their age. Decisions about running their businesses are based on different things – health, for instance, or the desire to do something different, but that could happen at any age.

It's only natural, as we near a big birthday, to think about reviewing our lives. We're aware of the losses of youth, beauty, being a mother to our children (even if they're still at home, they won't see you any more as the centre of their universe), loss of our parents for many (and certainly strong parents who can protect you) and opportunities. If we dwell on all of this, we'll become despondent although that doesn't mean we shouldn't acknowledge that some things have passed.

Instead, why not make a mental list of all the things gained in the previous five decades – an insight into life, for example, knowledge and experience, great friends and relationships, amazing places, myriad skills, interesting careers? In short, why not celebrate what matters in life, what we believe and why? You know who you are, you're comfortable in your skin and you're confident enough to say what you want. In short, you're less a slave to what everyone else thinks – and that's a very liberating feeling.

There's also much to which you can look forward. Katherine Whitehorn, writing recently in the *Guardian*, came up with a startling confession. 'I have lately discovered the joys of helplessness,' she wrote, while acknowledging that she has fought the cause for women all her life and has ferociously defended the position that she can do anything. But now, if there's something heavy to carry, she just waits until 'some muscles arrive' and asks for help. Why, she asked, has it taken her so long to work this out? And isn't it rather nice to be offered a seat on the bus when you are tired or being served first at meal times or being asked for your advice as a wise woman?

Let's get back to you and your birthday. A very useful activity to undertake if you're feeling reflective, and a much better alternative to letting your mind wallow in the negatives (see Question 5 in this section which discusses over-worrying) is to actively re-frame your concerns.

EXERCISE: ENJOYING THE NEXT STAGE

1. Find a piece of paper and somewhere to sit where you can be comfortable.

2. Remember a special event, a really lovely memory, one where you were completely relaxed. (See Question 2 of this section.) Write it down.

3. Now, in your mind, come back to today and list the things that are worrying you about being 60. Prioritise them.

4. Choose one to work on. My advice is to choose something that is relatively easy to start with.

5. Write a paragraph about the current problem or issue that is troubling you. You can do it in note form and should spend no longer than five minutes on it. Make sure to include your true emotions.

6. Now go back and explore your special memory for a few minutes, again making sure that you take note of your emotions.

7. Hold those thoughts and feelings. Then go back to the current problem and focus on the possible solutions.

8. Write down the solutions and try them out by concentrating on them as though you were there. See how you feel and think now.

9. Decide which solution is your favourite and when you're going to carry it out. Fix a date with yourself and a treat you'll give yourself when it's done.

You say that you didn't enjoy your fiftieth birthday and yet that being 50 has on the whole been all right. Is this because anniversaries in themselves are hard? Or is it the anticipation that something major will happen on that day and nothing will be the same afterwards? If you didn't focus on your birthday when you did the exercise above, repeat it now, making the particular day itself the problem.

So now what should you do to really enjoy it? This is your day to do whatever you want with whoever you like. It's entirely up to you. The following exercise should help you decide.

EXERCISE: HAPPY BIRTHDAYS

1. Think of your three best birthdays and run a video of them in your head.

2. What were the ingredients that made them good? Jot them down.

3. Now think of three birthdays you've been to that were fantastic. What were the winning ingredients in these? Write them down.

4. Now take a new sheet of paper and write all the ingredients down one side, leaving a space between each one.

5. Take a further piece of paper and write down all the things you really enjoy doing. Write them down five times. Cut each of these into pieces with one on each piece.

6. Go back to your list and match the activities with the ingredients.

7. Now choose the one that will give you the most ingredients and, hey presto, you have the perfect birthday treat!

   This may sound a long way to go about it but it'll be worth it.

One word of advice: people can become very excited about other people's big birthdays – especially family members – and assume the most wonderful thing in the world is to give them a surprise party. If that's your thing, fine. If not, let them know so they don't go to all that effort and find you cross or disappointed.

It's also all right to say what level of surprise you want. You may not need to know where you're going or who's going to be there but it could be useful to know how to dress. It's your day and the start of a great new decade.

Q4 **I've never been that interested in exercise. And yet, I'm continuously told that the older you are, the more important it is. I'm not sure I totally believe it. However, I do know I'm not as fit as I could be. I joined a gym one January and promised myself I'd go. I wasted a lot of money! I know I should change my habits, but how do I do this?**

It seems that it would be easier for you not to believe rather than to have to do it! Sadly, judging by all the research, I'm afraid it's true: exercise is good for you. But don't just take it from me. The 1996 WHO report, *Physical activity through transport as part of daily activities*, reported that participation in regular, moderate physical activity can delay functional decline. Older people, especially post-menopausal women, have a specific need to continue regular, rhythmic, weight-bearing, physical activity to preserve bone density and the integrity of muscle function and physical confidence that are essential if we're to avoid falls and consequent hip fractures.

So what does exercise do for us? It's good for our bodies, minds and social wellbeing. Physiologically, in the short term, it regulates our blood glucose levels, reducing the likelihood of diabetes and stimulating production of endorphins which combat stress. It improves the quality and quantity of sleep and improves our blood lipid profile so that cholesterol levels are reduced along with the risk of heart attacks.

Long term, there will be substantial improvements in all aspects of cardiovascular functioning, improvements in muscle strength helping you to maintain your shape, increased suppleness and flexibility to assist your stamina, balance and coordination. This, in turn, will reduce the incidence of falls, arthritic pain and achy joints while improving bone density and gastrointestinal transit time. It will also reduce the likelihood of colon cancer.

Exercise helps reduce anxiety and your general wellbeing will improve as endorphins are released into your body, making you feel full of vitality. The likelihood of depression decreases and it appears natural growth hormones stimulate new brain-cell production. This will improve thinking skills and the ability to make decisions. Reaction times will remain good, something that's essential if you're driving a car, for instance. Your ability to learn new skills will also remain undiminished which will encourage a feeling of self-worth and self-confidence.

There are no forms of exercise that are considered unsuitable for older people, provided that the exercise is tailored towards your level of fitness and takes into account any health problems you may have. If you haven't done much for a while, you should start slowly and build up. One perfect form of self-sabotage is to go for it hell for leather, strain every muscle, feel lousy and then convince yourself you're justified in giving it up! Doctors recommend 30 minutes a day of activity that stimulates the heart and lungs – that means cardiovascular exercise.

Try dance, yoga, Pilates, t'ai chi (and other martial arts) and gym sessions. Swimming, walking and cycling can be done alone or in groups, and group sports such as golf, racquet sports and even netball! There are also non-sporting activities, some of which you might do already. Just put in a little more effort and do them regularly and you'll soon feel the benefit. Examples include walking the dog, gardening, using the stairs instead of the lift, cycling to the shop for the daily paper, dancing to the radio, activities with grandchildren (frisbees, kites, balls), walking to the next bus stop or getting off a stop earlier, rowing a boat at the park – even enjoying more frequent sex!

When we first arrive in this world, we're born habit-free. We have instinctive reflexes such as swallowing and breathing. We cry when we're uncomfortable, alerting someone's attention. We learn that crying is a useful bit of behaviour because it gets our needs met. Many young children cry whenever they're slightly put out. But at some stage in our early lives we 'unlearn' this and replace the no-longer-useful habit with a different form of behaviour. That requires practice. If we're rewarded with positive feedback, it encourages us to continue and so we've learnt a new habit.

All our experiences are stored in our brain although we're not aware of most of them. If I ask you now to think of a green giraffe eating pink leaves, you'll gather from your unconscious mind all the relevant words and construct a picture. The giraffe is now in your conscious mind when it wasn't earlier. Our brain is triggered by all sorts of stimuli and lost pictures, thoughts and feelings can reappear at will. We hear a piece of music we haven't heard for years and the boyfriend we had at the time springs to mind. If we liked him and the recollection of the relationship is a happy one, we feel good. If he hurt us, we get in touch with those feelings and feel sad.

A good example to explain this is to think about how you learnt to ride a bike. There was a time when you didn't know what a bicycle was, you had no interest in it and, as a result, you were unconsciously incompetent. One day, you noticed that others were having fun on this machine. It looked easy so you had a go. You probably couldn't even get on and, once you did, you probably fell off. You became consciously incompetent.

You were then taught how to ride and, as long as you concentrated hard and no one spoke to you, you eventually mastered the art. You were now consciously competent. In time, you were able to cycle along, talk to your friends and look at the sights.

You were now unconsciously competent. The skill was integrated into your unconscious skill set, something you never forgot. To learn anything, we go through these four stages and, once it is truly learnt, our response becomes a habit with the result that we don't need to consciously think about it any more.

Take a moment and think of some of the habits you've acquired – for example, always double-locking the front door when you go out or putting your work bag away in a certain place before doing anything else. Our habits become so much a part of us that we don't think about them. If challenged, we'll defend them because we believe they represent the right way to think and behave.

Many of our habits can be extremely useful, like brushing our teeth every morning without having to leave ourselves a note! This automatic behaviour leaves space in our head to think about other things. Where a problem can arise is that we don't consciously decide which is a good habit and which is not and whether what was useful when we were 3 is useful when we're 53. These unconscious automatic behaviour patterns don't change on their own; we have to actively and consciously unlearn them. We also have to replace them with a new behaviour otherwise we'll just revert to the old habit. Anyone who has kicked the habit of smoking or putting sugar in their tea knows what I'm talking about.

But even when we know it's for health reasons, it still feels hard sometimes to break old habits because it requires changing our hard-wiring. If you're going to succeed, you need to have a positive goal and be very clear what the benefits are. What stops you doing exercise at the moment? Is it because you forget and suddenly it's midnight and bedtime? Or is it because you can't see the value? I hope you'll now agree that the real benefits are well worth it in keeping you feeling fit, healthy and young.

Don't set yourself an unrealistic goal like going swimming five times a week because you'll fall at the first hurdle. Start small. It takes up to 20 times to change a habit so walking to the station once won't help! It could help to leave a note in the car that tells you to walk to the station. And reward yourself for doing well. If you're walking, not driving, you'll be saving both petrol and the environment. So save the petrol money and buy yourself something you wouldn't have been able to afford. Eventually, you'll walk to the station without even taking a sidelong glance at the car.

And that's how a new habit is born.

Q5   As I get older, I worry more. If something minor happens, I assume it'll develop into a disaster. I've never learnt techniques for managing stress because I never thought I was prone to it! But I think I am now. What can I do?

I wonder what propelled you into thinking like this. Very often, there's a trigger that starts us on this route and we then get caught in a spiral of negative thinking and anxiety. Think back and see if you can identify an event where something did go wrong or, even if it was rectified, it unnerved you in some way.

My hunch is that getting older has made you feel more vulnerable and less in control so that the consequences of something bad happening will be harder to shrug off. For example: 'If I fall, I'm more likely to break a bone and then I'll be off work and short of cash. But I need to go for food. I could ask one of my children although that might make them see me as older and, anyway, I don't want to be dependent on them.' And so on and so on. Does this sound familiar to you?

We behave when we're in this kind of state as though we have no control over our thoughts. This type of thinking is a habit. Habits can be formed after just one event although they take longer to stop. (See the previous question.) The thought habit – in your case that things will probably go wrong – becomes the norm. One of my clients who, much like you, had not been a worrier became understandably anxious when she heard there had been a train crash on a route that one of her children used regularly at the time. Fortunately for her, her child wasn't on the train but this triggered an anxiety thought pathway and she found herself obsessed with any family member's daily travels. This was taking over her life. By identifying the cause, she was able to put it back into perspective and get on with her life.

There are times when we're right to react strongly because something has happened and it's difficult and painful. Problems occur, though, when we react more strongly than is appropriate for the event. Our brain is full of our chatter. What if x happens or y? And on we go. Usually, we associate with these events as though we were there. (See Section 1, Question 3.) Our bodies, not knowing any better, get ready to deal with the impending disaster and our flight or fight mechanisms get activated.

As they have nothing concrete to respond to, they turn inwards and we become stressed and can start feeling unwell. (See the Emergency Relaxation Technique exercise on p.180.) The result is that we're left unable to deal with our ordinary life, let alone a real disaster. And, even though we know this in our rational mind, it seems impossible at the time to remain in control of our emotions.

Many of us think that the best way to make decisions and process information is to keep turning over whatever it is that is troubling us. We worry that, if we stop thinking, we'll forget what we need to do. The fact is that we think using both the conscious and unconscious part of our brains. Because we can't tangibly reach the unconscious bit, we assume that the only part that works is the conscious one and, therefore, to solve the issue, we need to be aware of it all of the time.

If you have two thoughts in your head at once while you're talking, you'll invariably find that you become tongue-tied. Our conscious brain can't process too much at once. However, our unconscious mind is very good at doing just that and we need to learn to trust it. One useful trick is to leave things alone in our heads for a while and get on consciously with something else. When you return to the problem, you may be surprised to discover you've got the answer.

A further danger when we have got into this spiral is that thinking of one minor worry triggers off another, loosely connected worry which multiplies out of all proportion. It's important, therefore, when we're worrying, to identify if there's anything we can do about it. If there is, then being relaxed so you can coolly and calmly come to a solution is essential. If you're in a high state of angst, the answer will elude you. If you can't do anything about it, you need a break. Put it aside and return to it at a later date.

The following process will help you do this.

EXERCISE: MANAGING OUR WORRIES

1. Check out if this is an actual disaster you have to deal with and your response is appropriate – for example, if there's water pouring through the kitchen ceiling which requires your immediate attention.

2. If, however, you're worrying that the report you wrote at work may not be good enough, or a friend may not have liked the present you gave her for her birthday, say,. 'STOP', to yourself loudly and clearly.

3. If you worry you'll lose what you're trying to work out, write it down. This will distance you from the problem and allow you to let it go.

4. Decide if this is something worth your consideration or an unnecessary worry that's just worry for its own sake. If the former, agree with yourself a time when you'll revisit it and make a decision; if the latter, drop it!

5. Now focus on stopping your thinking. If you're going to succeed, you need to put something else in its place. You can't just leave a blank. Think of something that makes you feel good. Do something different – physical exercise is great. Go for a walk if you can't get to the gym or do some gardening or cooking. Watch the telly or put on music or read a good book. This is where iPods are great as you can plug yourself in and no one else can intrude. Audio tapes are fantastic at getting you involved and taking your thoughts elsewhere.

6. When you come back to your problem, plan a strategy for dealing with it. Do you need to talk to someone else for some help? Do you need to break the problem down so you're clear what you're worrying about and which bits can be solved? Plan a problem-solving strategy and stick to it. (See Section 1, Question 5.)

Many women get into the habit in their friendships of talking about problems. It makes us feel close and intimate with our peers although this can, at times, be less than helpful because it perpetuates the problem by constantly referring to it. If your friends are talking to you about the same thing again and again and you haven't moved anywhere with it, stop discussing it. The friend who's in a bad relationship, who tells you every day what her partner has done but still stays there, is not being helped by you listening. Offering to help her if she plans to leave or do something different to improve her situation is fine but joining the spiral path is less than helpful.

Sometimes, we get into a worry pattern because we're tired and it becomes a vicious circle. We're worried so we don't sleep and then become too tired to cope and too overtired to sleep. When we sleep, we give our body and brain a rest and allow our unconscious time to work things out. Most of us have had the experience of going to bed not knowing the answer and waking up with one.

As we don't function as well when tired, we develop symptoms such as memory loss, clumsiness, aches and pains and foggy, unclear thinking. All of these are similar symptoms to those seen in some old people. If we're already anxious about getting older, this anxiety will merely exacerbate the feeling that we're old and deteriorating. The truth is that maybe we're just tired. Hence the need for quality sleep.

Tips to help you sleep:

- Do some exercise every day (not just before bed). Exercise uses energy and our body responds by wanting to replenish itself for the next day.

- Don't eat or drink just before you go to bed.

- If you can't sleep, get up and do some relaxation exercises. Take in three deep breaths through your nose, then breathe out through your mouth. Breathe in and tighten the muscles in your feet as you breathe out, relaxing the muscles. Repeat three times. Now do exactly the same with your ankle muscles, followed by your calf muscles, thighs, tummy, chest, hands, wrists, forearms, upper arms, shoulders, neck, face, eyes and top of your head. You'll feel appreciably calmer at the completion of this routine. Avoid the TV as it may well wake you up.

- Try to get into a routine so you have approximately the same amount of time in bed each night. We are habitual creatures.

- Make sure you're warm. This helps the blood vessels dilate and the body to settle down.

- If your mind still isn't calm, listen to a story tape or music as you drift off to help your brain slow down.

If you follow these suggestions, you will find that on the whole you have positive thoughts and feelings and life will seem so much easier. (See Question 2 in this section.)

Q6 **There's no denying it: I'm more forgetful than I used to be. I hear a story from someone and forget the main points; I lose my glasses and my keys; I forget people's names. I have an idea in my head that just disappears. And yet, I'm only 56. I'm worried about my memory. Does everyone's memory deteriorate? What can I do to keep it honed?**

At the risk of being shouted down by you, I'm not sure it's a fact that our memory deteriorates because we're in our fifties. Of course, debilitating diseases such as Alzheimer's and dementia leave people with no memory to speak of and they can sometimes affect people in their fifties although, thankfully, that's reasonably rare. If the blood supply to brain tissue is poor, e.g. when there is a clot or haemorrhage, the amount of oxygen received is reduced and this will cause damage and the outcome may be memory loss.

This does not usually happen in the brain of a fit and healthy person in their fifties or sixties. We do lose a number of brain cells as we get older but very few in proportion to the ones that remain and the reality is that we've anyway been losing a few since we were approximately sixteen! As we get old, our long-term memory gets clearer while our short-term may suffer.

Anyone who has worked with or lived with young people would be hard-pushed to beat them on the forgetting stakes – PE kit, passports, parents' birthdays, papers for an important meeting, house keys, provisional driving licence needed for a driving test . . . The list is endless. The difference, though, is that they laugh it off and we don't! We worry. We tend to notice it more and I think assume we're forgetting things because we've been told that this is what happens when you get to our age.

But forgetting is different from memory loss.

I'm not dismissing the fact you're concerned about forgetting names, your keys, glasses and so on. Most of us do that. But, truthfully, were you someone who never did this before? Thought not! Of course, if it feels significantly different and it's causing you concern, go and see your GP. My hunch, though, is that it's probably due to a number of factors, most of which you can eliminate.

First and foremost are the beliefs we hold. If we believe that as we get older our memory will begin to deteriorate, then every time we forget something, we'll blame it on our advancing years. What's more, if that's what we think is the explanation, it'll become another self-fulfilling prophecy.

In 1956, George Miller, a psychologist, published his theory that a person could only hold an average of seven items in their head at any one time. All of us, whatever our age, have had experiences where we've gone into a room and wondered what we were doing there; or put the keys down somewhere safe and temporarily lost them; or forgotten to take a vital piece of paper with us. In our busy lives, most of us try to hold more than our natural capacity of information in our brains. Another factor that has a huge effect on our memory is stress. Worry affects our ability to remember and can prematurely age our brains. I've talked about worry in Question 5 of this section. The physiological responses are useful when there's a real danger but not when there isn't. (See Section 4, Question 11.) There's evidence that some of the chemical reactions associated with stress such as the production of glucocorticoids has an effect on the ageing of brain cells and the brain's ability to make new connections. Stress ages the brain. It creates the same behaviours we equate with ageing – in other words, we become forgetful.

The other debilitating factor is tiredness. When we're exhausted, we're unable to function as effectively. We become clumsy and forgetful and inarticulate. Many of us have stayed up late to finish something and come back to it in the morning to find we hadn't done our best piece of work. Having said all of that, worrying about our memory is the worst thing we can do for it. If we accept that there'll be times when we're forgetful, there are techniques to help us remember things.

The brain is a remarkable organ, constantly capable of learning throughout life. So, the more active we keep it, the more likely it is to remain healthy. We all know of remarkable people who are still working in their nineties. Although some would say that, by doing this, we can prevent diseases such as Alzheimer's, I'm not convinced there's yet enough evidence to be sure. What I do know, however, is that there's no doubt that keeping the brain active and stimulated will keep it functioning pretty well.

We acquire most of our knowledge when we're young. Children never stop asking questions and filling their minds with information. Giving yourself a few hours a week to learn something new as you get older provides fantastic food for your brain. You may not become a concert pianist but you're never too old to learn an instrument – or how to throw a pot or ice a cake.

Tony Buzan, in his book *Age-proof Your Brain: Sharpen Your Memory in 7 Days*, has lots of exercises you can do to stimulate your brain. It is worth doing some research and finding some mind exercises you might enjoy. Many people have become addicted to word-search games and Suduko – perfect ways to exercise the mind!

You mention you have a brilliant idea and then it's gone. A lot of us find this occurs in the middle of the night or when we're relaxing. It's well known that the resting mind often comes up with solutions. Keep a notepad by your bed or in your handbag so you can jot down ideas. Many an explorer and writer have done this so they can capture their observations.

Use mnemonics to remember things – for example, the names of the daughters of a friend: Gail, Iris, Rosemary and Lily – by thinking of the word 'girl'! Forgetting people's names is very common. We've all experienced that embarrassing moment when we meet someone we saw only the day before and our mind goes blank. One of the tips for remembering names (or any information) is to say it and hear it at least three times in quick succession. Ask them their name and then repeat it to them and then use it as much as you can in the conversation without sounding daft and say their name when you say goodbye. We tend to remember the first and last bits more than the middle. Another aid is to attach a picture to their name: if their name is Rose, think of red cheeks or, if their name is Mickey, think of a mouse! But remember, we can only hold on to seven bits of information at once. One of the tricks for not forgetting things in absent-minded moments is to train yourself to scan. Recall the 'picture' of your conversation and then, if it's important, make notes of what was said afterwards.

Easier said than done but give it a try and don't be too hard on yourself.

Q7 I came across you when I was surfing the net. I'm 59 and have very little to complain about, but I still feel low about my age. I'm aware that my body is not quite how it was. I suffer the odd aches and pains of anyone my age. But it often feels like I've no one to discuss this with. When I was younger, I went to women's groups and, when I had my children, I went to pre-birth groups, then groups for toddlers and so on where we women all had a good chat (and moan) about everything! So, why do we end up hiding ourselves and our feelings at this stage of our lives? It just doesn't seem cool to talk about ageing, the menopause and all the rest of it.

A number of the answers in this book talk about our bodies as we age and so I'm going to focus on the second part of your question about hiding ourselves, something that preoccupies many women of your age. Do take a look at Section 3, Question 3 and Section 2, Question 1.

There are lots of reasons we don't talk about these things. One of the main reasons is that being a postmenopausal woman is a relatively modern phenomenon. A hundred years ago, the average age of the menopause was 47 and the average life expectancy was 49. Now, most women are just over 50 when they become menopausal and can expect to live a lot longer. The previous generations of women, our grandmothers' and mothers', were not mostly ones for talking openly about women's issues and their feelings. It wasn't their fault but they didn't represent good role models. (Most of us can remember where we got our sex education and it wasn't from our parents!)

As a group, therefore, we've pioneered the talking about puberty, sex and relationships and, I agree with you, we do seem to have gone a little quiet. I think it's because, up till now, it hasn't looked as though the next stage was going to be too much fun. The baby boomers are the ones who have to put all this stuff on the map.

I was recently asked to comment on some new government services, targeted at the 50+. It's too easy to lump everyone above that age in the same bracket and yet, no one would ever ask you to devise services for the 10–40 age group. Although there may be some issues in common for the over-fifties, such as early retirement or certain health issues, that's about the extent of the similarities.

Zoë Williams undertook a study for the *Guardian* newspaper in 2006. Wearing a prosthetic face of a woman 34 years her senior, she went out into the world. She didn't change her stance or her voice but was nonetheless shocked by the reaction she encountered. No one noticed her until she spoke and then they were surprised she was so noisy. Not only does our body become older but, apparently, we're expected to occupy less space. As women, we've always done that. Think of men who often sit with their arms and legs splayed out when relaxing or in a meeting – no woman does that. As we get older, we become even smaller in every sense and less noticeable. All the more reason to make *lots* of noise!

Many of us are beginning to talk in small intimate groups and laugh about ourselves. When we do, we often focus on things that aren't so special such as bladder control and leaking when laughing, constantly having to go to the loo which wakes us up in the night and then we suffer from lack of sleep: hair in places we never used to have it, hot flushes and being irritable with everyone, and avoiding sex in case a hot flush occurs halfway through!

Part of the blame can be laid at the door of the cosmetics industry. From an early age we're bombarded with products to fight the ageing process as though it's some battle doomed to failure. At some point in our fifties or sixties, we're expected to give in and start to look our age. We're meant to stop keeping up with fashion and stay dressed very much as we did at the point we gave in.

Having said all that, I think things really are changing. Look at Dove's 2007 advertisement campaign celebrating real women. Just changing the language so we have cosmetics that are deemed pro-age rather than anti-age helps to change society's thinking. We need to start talking differently. Rather than cry with despair when we see a grey hair or a hair in the wrong place on our chin, we should feel proud to be maturing in body as in mind. We never complain that we're wiser, more skilled and experienced yet we complain about our looks and our bodies.

Susie Orbach, a psychoanalyst who's written about women's issues over the last 30 years, worked with Dove on their project, 'Beauty Comes of Age'. She says, 'You'd never know that women like me . . . existed from today's media. We're almost invisible and if we are visible then we are supposed to be trying to pass for younger . . . and try to reflect those women – in their mid to late thirties – who are in the anti-ageing advertisements, selling us a mantra that age can be defied.' The findings of the study suggest that only 2 per cent of young women believe sexiness is still possible once a woman hits 50 and only 1 out of 5 women over 50 believe they are sexy.

Germaine Greer famously wrote in *The Change: Women, Aging and the Menopause* about women becoming invisible once their sexuality diminished. With so many women in their fifties and sixties enjoying their sexuality and sexual freedom post-childbearing, this statement needs to be overturned, but we still have a way to go.

One of the reasons women get ignored by men and younger women is because men, and particularly younger males, simply don't know how to talk to us. We're too old to be bedmates and too wise to patronise so they get stuck and say nothing at all. Educating our young men to talk to older women who aren't their mothers or their friends' mothers is one of our challenges. I also think we get stuck and tend to quiz the young about their achievements and what they're doing rather than just chat. Few of us learn to interact with older people who we aren't either related to or who are our boss. We're not interested in ageing until we're ageing! I think this will change as there are so many more people in their fifties and sixties and it is the subject of many fiction and non-fiction books.

For many of us, until we get to being *un*-noticed, we're unaware how much we relied on our youth for attention. I'm not suggesting we want to be leered at but it would be nice for people to be aware of us, to open the odd door, to smile and acknowledge us occasionally. Once we feel invisible, we often exacerbate the situation. Seemingly innocent actions such as a barperson serving two other people first can prompt us to complain and risk being branded 'grumpy old women', another title we're trying to avoid.

A survey undertaken on www.menopausematters.co.uk found that very few women even talk to their doctors about menopausal matters, preferring to access their information from the internet. This menopause site gets over 1.5 million hits per month. But all is not lost. We're beginning to make a noise about ourselves. Look at *Menopause the Musical*, which came to London in 2007. It was slated by British critics and I accept that it may not have been the slickest show in town but I wonder if the subject didn't have a lot to do with it.

Things are also changing with actors like Helen Mirren, Meryl Streep, Joanna Lumley and Judi Dench, all of them in their late fifties or older and each one being hailed as sexy and vibrant. So, we may have bordered on the invisible up to now but we can change that and become the generation which shouts about the benefits of being 50+ women and goes on making a noise well into our eighties. That way, the cultural norm will change.

Viva the 50+!

Over to You ...

The older we get, the more questions we seem to have. We learn by looking for the answers to our questions. As is apparent from the numerous questions I receive about this stage of our lives, there are many more questions both to be asked and answered.

To this end, I've set up a question and answer service so we can continue this dialogue. Please send your questions to my website: www.experiencematters.org.uk.

Every week, I will answer one question online and also post a couple more seeking advice interactively. A problem shared is a problem solved and more heads than one gets us there faster.

If you want more personal advice, you'll be directed to telephone coaching from myself or an Experience Matters coach, and other sources of support.

I really look forward to hearing from you.

Take care and enjoy!

Keren

Resource Lists

General resources

www.50connect.co.uk
Information, articles and links
to other sites

Finance, health,
travel, food and
drink, genealogy, plus
many other topics.

www.ageconcern.org.uk
The UK's largest organisation
working with and for older people

Local services, book-
shop, fact sheets,
telephone informa-
tion line on health,
housing, income,
pensions, etc.

www.age-matters.org
An international site
with useful links

They are committed
to wellbeing and
designed to provide
easy access to advice,
information, products
and services.

www.agething.co.uk
Comprehensive site for the 50+
(formerly www.fiftyon.co.uk)

Offers information on
work, life, a forum
and self-help ideas.

www.armchairadvice.co.uk
Advice and information, plus
services directory

Information on
relationships, employ-
ment, law advice,
death, bereavement
and loss.

www.bbc.co.uk
Information and links to many areas

Care, saving and
investments, facts
about ageing,
housing, leisure,
health, etc.

www.businessballs.com
Free ethical learning and development
resource for people and organisations,
run by Alan Chapman

Information on many
topics and personal
development, self-
and organisational
development.

www.direct.gov.uk/en/over50s
Government website for services
for the 50+

A very useful portal
site for the over-
fifties. Covers all
areas.

www.enjoy50plus.co.uk
Directory of resources for the 50+

Useful site to find
solutions and infor-
mation.

www.experiencematters.org.uk
Coaching and consultancy for the 50+

A consultancy that
specialises in issues
affecting the 50+.

Experience Matters offers coaching sessions, information and guidance to enable individuals to find solutions for all issues affecting the 50+ at home and work. Includes EFT sessions and HBDI profiling.

www.hairnet.org
Now called Digital Unite. British specialists in digital inclusion for older people

Helps individuals, communities and organisations who need IT skills and ensures they can use IT for their specific needs.

www.ksa.org.uk
Keren Smedley Associates Training and consultancy company

Management and work solutions for organisations and coaching for individuals.

www.laterlife.com
Useful site even if not 50+ or 60+ as has ideas for gifts and so on related to older life

Contains a wealth of references, ideas and features to help enjoy later life to the full.

www.lifes4living.co.uk
Comprehensive site for all issues

Website and club for people over 50.

www.mables.org.uk
It is a one-stop resource for whatever the 50+ need to help make the most of life

Healthcare, well-being, advice, cosmetics, dating, money, etc.

www.maturetimes.co.uk
The voice of your generation

Articles on a wide variety of topics affecting the older person.

www.nhsdirect.nhs.uk
General information on health and emotional issues. A 24-hour telephone helpline

Empty nest, menopause, ageing and general health issues.

www.over50s.com
Comprehensive site for all issues

The New Generation, the silver surfer and the over-50 age group.

www.overfiftieswebsites.co.uk
List of websites for the 50+

Covers finance, hobbies, holidays, etc., and general information for the over-fifties.

www.saga.co.uk
Magazine and organisation for the 50+

Covers all areas of life, insurance, travel, health, etc.

www.silversurfers.net
Links to everything you
would ever need

Wide range of infor-
mation, including
health section, holi-
days, finance, food,
homes, etc.

www.statistics.gov.uk
Government website

Age composition,
marriage, births,
divorce and statistics.

www.uk-overfiftiesdirectory.co.uk
A selected directory of UK
over-fifties links

Lists and links to
many useful sites on
a variety of subjects.

www.visiblewomen.co.uk
The site for women who enjoy
being younger at 50

Offers information
on most issues
affecting the 50+
woman.

www.wikipedia.org
A free encyclopaedia

Very useful (though
not always 100 per
cent accurate) infor-
mation with links to
useful sites.

❧ Section One ❧

Additional resources

See the General Resource List.

www.breastcancercare.org.uk
Support with breast cancer

UK's leading provider of information, practical assistance and emotional support.

www.cancerbackup.org.uk
Cancer information service

Europe's leading cancer information service, providing accurate, up-to-date and authoritative cancer information, resources and support.

www.edwdebono.com
Relates to Edward de Bono's work on thinking tools

Information for all ages and occupations.

www.life-academy.co.uk
Managing change and life from mid-life

A national centre for life planning, helping individuals prepare for the next stage.

www.macmillan.org.uk
Support with cancer

Provides expert information with practical and emotional support.

www.retirementexpert.co.uk
How to make the most of your retirement

Useful information, features and practical advice.

✦ Section Two ✦

Additional resources

See the General Resource List.

www.baaps.org.uk
British Association of Aesthetic Plastic Surgeons

Clear information with pluses and risks.

www.dh.gov.uk/en/policyandguidance/healthandsocial-caretopics/cosmeticsurgery
Information on cosmetic surgery and non-surgical cosmetic treatments

Gives non-biased information to help make an informed decision about whether to have surgery or non-surgical treatments.

www.doveproage.com
Dove's campaign to show
images of older women

Information on
ageing and its effect
on the body.

www.emofree.com
Gary Craig's site for Emotional
Freedom Technique

A wealth of material
and a free manual to
download.

www.fashionpeople.co.uk
A website run by *Saga* magazine's
fashion consultants

Personal shoppers,
fashion consultants
and makeover
experts.

www.ivillage.co.uk
The website for women

Beauty and other
issues affecting the
older woman.

www.wlbeauty.com
The website of an independent image
consultant and one of Saga's
expert coaches

Information on
anti-ageing skincare,
cosmetic surgery and
all beauty treatments.

๛ Section Three ๏

Additional resources

See the General Resource List.

www.amarantmenopausetrust.co.uk
A charity for women going through
the menopause

Set up in 1980 to
provide information
and advice. Also has
a telephone helpline.

www.fiftyalready.com
Dating site

Join free and meet
thousands like you!

www.gaystheword.co.uk
Lesbian and gay bookshop

An independent
bookshop for inde-
pendent thinkers.

www.laterlifedating.com
Relationships

A specialist service
for over-fifties
relationships.

www.match.com
Online dating site with very
good reviews

Successful site with
safety tips, etc., infor-
mation and articles.

www.mothers35plus.com
Site for the older mother

Wealth of information
including statistics.

www.mothersover40.com
A site for the older mother

All the issues that confront the older parent.

www.oloc.org
Old Lesbians Organising for Change

For the 60+, specifically called 'old' to challenge it being seen as a negative term.

www.patrasilk.com
Mail-order firm for stylish underwear

Site for all ages but with good ideas for the older person.

www.perfectmatch.com
Online dating site

A popular site which offers highly compatible matches and advanced search tools.

www.pinktherapy.com
UK's largest independent therapy organisation working with gender and sexual minority groups

They aim to promote high-quality therapy and training services for people who are lesbian, gay, bisexual and transsexual.

www.primesingles.net
A dating site that has a 50+ section and is widely used

Meet friends and make relationships.

www.relate.org.uk
Advice, support and counselling
for managing relationships

Information, plus
counselling directory.

www.styledash.com
Details of a number of lingerie
companies that cater for the
older person

Lingerie line 'Zoro'
for the 35 to 60+

www.womyn.org
Directory of sites for lesbian women

Covers a wide variety
of areas including
relationships, commu-
nities and holidays.

❧ Section Four ❧

Additional resources

See the General Resource List.

www.eng.aeweb.org
Ageing and ethnicity website

Worldwide informa-
tion on issues related
to minority ethnic
older persons.

www.alzheimers.org.uk
Alzheimer's Society. A leading care
and research charity for people with
all types of dementia, their families
and carers

Information about
different forms of
dementia, help for
carers, news and
events.

www.fpa.co.uk

Family planning service, a registered charity working to improve sexual health and reproductive rights for all people

Information on sexual matters and services.

www.grandparents-association.org.uk

Dedicated to raising grandparents' consciousness

Provides support to enable the relationship between grandchildren and grandparents to flourish.

www.grandparentsplus.org.uk

Aims to raise the profile of grandparents and the extended family as providers of care

Supports grandparents and research information.

www.helptheaged.org.uk

Help the Aged charity

Advice services for older people and their carers.

www.netdoctor.co.uk/womenshealth

Comprehensive site for all health issues

Information on many of the issues affecting women, plus an interactive site.

www.webofloneliness.com

Information on loneliness

Links to a number of sites including those offering emotional support.

∽ Section Five ∾

Additional resources

See the General Resource List.

www.agepositive.gov.uk
A government site, useful for
employers and employees

Information, advice
and case studies
around age discrimi-
nation and rights in
employment.

www.attractingabundance.com
Offers tools for attracting abundance
using EFT

Ideas as to how to
attract success by
clearing limiting
beliefs and releasing
resistance.

www.eftdownunder.com
Australian site with information
on energy therapies

Information on EFT,
simple energy tech-
niques (SET) and
proactive therapy
(PET).

www.gapadvice.org
For independent 'gap' information

Has a section on
career breaks and
retirement breaks
and offers an
advisory service.

www.grownupgapyear.co.uk
Gap-year travel for grown-ups.
Can be for shorter periods.

Wealth of information on where to go, how to get organised, including financial advice.

www.moneyfacts.co.uk
General independent website for all ages with a section for over-fifties

Personal finance advice.

www.niace.org.uk
A non-governmental organisation promoting adult learning

Learning and useful links for older adults from all walks of life and ability.

www.primeinitiative.org.uk
National organisation dedicated to helping people over 50 set up in business

Wealth of information and support and networking events.

www.taen.org.uk
The Age Employment Network

Promotes an effective job market which works for people in mid- and later life.

www.u3a.org.uk
The Third Age Trust is the national representative body for the Universities of the Third Age (U3A)

U3As are self-help, self-managed life-long learning co-operatives for older people no longer in full-time work. Opportunities to pursue learning for fun.

www.volunteersabroad.com
Lists gap projects

Useful site to direct you to the appropriate organisation.

www.wiseowls.co.uk
Specialists in online recruitment for people over 45.

Voice of the baby boomer generation dedicated to tackling ageism. Offers work experience and advice.

www.workingcareers.com
Provides access to information, advice and services regarding career management and counselling

Help with all aspects of a career and has a downloadable guide for over-fifties job hunting.

www.wrinklies.org
Recruitment and employment agency specialising in placing older workers

They address the challenge to restore the balance in the workforce. Career advice and training.

❧ Section Six ❧

Additional resources

See the General Resource List.

www.50plus.org
Lifelong Fitness Alliance
advocates wellbeing

Offers information
on health and fitness.

www.50plushealth.co.uk
General 50+ health issues

Information on good
forms of exercise,
discussions, alternative
ideas and products, plus
some statistics.

www.bhf.org.uk
British Heart Foundation

Healthy eating, staying
active and preventing
heart disease.

www.buzancentres.com
Provides a wide range of learning
techniques to help improve memory

Lots of resources for
improving memory,
speed reading, increased
concentration, etc.

www.eatwell.gov.uk
Information on eating well from
the Food Standards Agency

Information on
Ashwell shape chart
and other diet informa-
tion and food labelling.
Has specific section for
older people.

www.hbdi.com
Herrman International founding
company for HBDI™

Information, online
survey and training.

www.hbdi-uk.com
Information on HBDI™

Information, online
survey and training.

www.nice.org.uk
National Institute for Health and
Clinical Excellence

Independent
organisation which
provides national guid-
ance on promoting good
health and treating ill
health.

www.patient.co.uk/showdoc/37
Section on senior health

Information leaflets,
patient support and self-
help groups, plus links
to numerous useful
sites.

www.ramblers.org.uk
Website with information about
walking, holidays and health with
section for the over-fifties

Hundreds of
affiliated sites with
local groups. Walking
for health ideas.

www.surgerydoor.co.uk
Comprehensive health and medicine
information

Covers a wide
variety of health areas
including online health
checks.

Bibliography

Ashton, Robert *The Life Plan: 700 Simple Ways to Change Your Life for the Better*, Pearson Education, 2006.

Bandler, Richard *Using Your Brain for a Change*, eds S. and C. Andreas, Real People Press US, 1985.

Barkley, Nella and Sandburg, Eric *The Crystal-Barkley Guide to Taking Charge of Your Career*, Workman Publishing, 1996.

Barusch, A. S. and Steen, P. 'Keepers of Community in a Changing World. Generations, Special Issue on Grandparenting at Century's End' in *Readings in Gerontological Nursing*, ed. C. Rector, Lippincott-Raven Publishers, 1996.

Berne, Eric *Games People Play – The Basic Handbook of Transactional Analysis,* Ballantine Books, new edn, 1996.

Berne, Eric *What Do You Say after You Say Hello?* Corgi, 1975.

Bevan, Rob and Wright, Tim *52 Brilliant Ideas – Unleash Your Creativity: Secrets of a Genius*, Infinite Ideas Ltd, revised edn, 2004.

Brown, Bobbi *Bobbi Brown Living Beauty*, Headline Springboard, 2007.

Brown, Sally *52 Brilliant Ideas – Live Longer: Your Whole Health Route to Longer Life*, Infinite Ideas Ltd, 2005.

Burns, David D. *Feeling Good Handbook*, Plume US, second revised edn, 2000.

Butler, R., Etcoff, N., Orbach, S. and D'Agostini, Heidi, 'Beauty Comes of Age: Findings of the 2006 Dove global study on aging, beauty and well-being,' *Dove*, 2006.

Butler-Bowden, Tom *50 Self-help Classics: 50 Inspirational Books to Transform Your Life from Timeless Sages to Contemporary Gurus*, Nicholas Brealey Publishing, 2003.

Buzan, Tony *The Buzan Skills Handbook: The Shortcut to Success in Your Studies with Mind Mapping, Speed Reading and Winning Memory Techniques*, BBC Active, 2006.

Buzan, Tony *Age-proof Your Brain: Sharpen Your Memory in 7 Days*, Harper Thorsons, 2007.

Buzan, Tony and Keene, Raymond *The Age Heresy*, Ebury Press, 1996.

Cameron, Julia *The Artist's Way*, Pan, 1997.

Carnegie, Dale *How to Win Friends and Influence People*, Vermilion, new edn, 2007.

Covey, Stephen R *The Seven Habits of Highly Effective People*, Simon & Schuster, revised edn, 2004.

Crowley, Chris, Lodge, Henry S. and Sheehy, Gail *Younger Next Year for Women: Turn Back Your Biological Clock*, Workman Publishing, 2005.

de Bono, Edward *Six Thinking Hats*, Penguin Books, second revised edn, 2000.

de Bono, Edward *Serious Creativity: Using the Power of Lateral Thinking to Create New Ideas*, HarperCollins, 1995.

Dench, Geoff and Ogg, Jim *Grandparenting in Britain: A Baseline Study*, Institute of Community Studies, 2002.

Dilits, Robert *Changing Belief Systems with Neuro-Linguistic Programming*, Meta Publications US, 1990.

Dooley, Michael and Stacey, Sarah *Your Change, Your Choice*, Hodder Mobius, 2006.

Ehrenfeld, Tom and Collins, Jim *The Startup Garden: How Growing a Business Grows You*, McGraw-Hill, 2001.

Feinstein, David, Eden, Donna and Craig, Garry *The Healing Power of EFT and Energy Psychology*, Piatkus, 2006.

Francina, Suza *The New Yoga for People Over 50: A Comprehensive Guide for Midlife and Older Beginners*, Health Communications, 1997.

Fraser, Eva *Eva Fraser's Facial Workout*, Penguin Books, 1992.

Gavin, Jeff *Internet Dating More Successful than Thought*, University of Bath, 2005.

Gawain, Shakti *Creative Visualisation and Meditation Exercises to*

Enrich Your Life, New World Library, second revised edn, 1997.

Goleman, Daniel *Emotional Intelligence*, Bloomsbury, 1996.

Gordon, W. J. J. *Synetics: The Development of Creative Capacity*, HarperCollins College Division, 1961.

Greer, Germaine *The Change: Women, Aging and the Menopause*, Random House, 1994.

Groves, Dawn *Stress Reduction for Busy People: Finding Peace in an Anxious World*, New World Library, 2004.

Harrold, Fiona *Be Your Own Life Coach: How to Take Control of Your Life and Achieve Your Wildest Dreams*, Coronet, 2001.

Hawkes, Nigel 'Sex, Sexuality and the Over-60s' in *The Times*, 2007.

Hay, Jack *Stay Fit and Fantastic Over 50*, Foulsham, 2003.

Hay, Louise L. *You Can Heal Your Life*, Full Circle Publishing, 2003.

Herrmann, Ned *The Whole Brain Business*, McGraw Hill, 1995.

Holden, Robert *Happiness Now!: Timeless Wisdom for Feeling Good Fast*, Hodder Mobius, 1999.

James, Muriel and Jongeward, Dorothy *Born to Win*, Da Capo Press, 1996.

Jeffers, Susan *Feel the Fear and Do It Anyway*, Vermilion, 2007.

Jeffers, Susan *The Little Book of Confidence*, Jeffers Press, 2005.

Kelsey, Linda *Fifty Is Not a Four-letter Word*, Hodder & Stoughton, 2007.

Kübler-Ross, Elisabeth *On Death and Dying*, Simon & Schuster, reprint edn, 1997.

Lindenfield, Gael *The Positive Woman: Simple Steps to Optimism and Creativity*, Harper Thorsons, 2000.

Look, Carol *Attracting Abundance with EFT*, AuthorHouse, 2005.

McClelland, David *Human Motivation*, Cambridge Press, 1988.

McGinty, Michelle, 'A New Wrinkle on the Anti-ageing Craze,' in the *Scotsman*, 2006.

Maslow, Abraham H. *Motivation and Personality*, Longman, third revised edn, 1987.

Middleton, John *Upgrade Your Brain: 52 Brilliant Ideas for Everyday Genius*, Infinite Ideas Ltd, 2006.

Mindgym, The *The Mindgym: Give Me Time*, Time Warner Books, 2006.

Morris, Monica *Falling in Love Again: The Mature Woman's Guide to Finding Romantic Fulfilment*, Square One Publishing, 2004.

Mula, Rose *The Stranger in My Mirror*, Writer's Showcase Press, 2003.

O'Connor, Joseph and Seymour, John *Introducing Neuro-Linguistic Programming: The New Psychology of Personal Excellence*, Aquarian Press, 1990.

Orbach, Susie and Eichenbaum, Luise *Bittersweet: Facing up to Feelings of Love, Envy and Competition in Women's Friendships*, Arrow Books, 1988.

Orbach, Susie and Eichenbaum, Luise *What Do Women Want?* HarperCollins, 2000.

Peele, Stanton with Brodsky, Archie *Love and Addiction*, Sphere, 1977.

Pinker, Steven *How the Mind Works*, Penguin Books, 1999.

Reid, Stephen *How to Think: Building Your Mental Muscle*, Pearson Education, 2002.

Righton, Caroline *The Life Audit*, Hodder Mobius, 2006.

Rogers, Steven *The Entrepreneur's Guide to Finance and Business: Wealth Creation Techniques for a Business*, McGraw-Hill, 2002.

Seligman, Martin E. P. *Learned Optimism: How to Change Your Mind and Life*, Vintage Books US, reprint edition, 2006.

Siler, Todd *Think Like a Genius*, Bantam, 1997.

Smedley, Keren and Whitten, Helen *Age Matters – Employing, Motivating and Managing Older Employees*, Gower, 2006.

Smith, Alistair *The Brain's Behind It*, Network Educational Press, 2004.

Snyder, C. R. and Lopez, S. J. eds *Handbook of Positive Psychology*, Oxford University Press, 2005.

Stoppard, Miriam *Defying Age: How to Think, Act and Stay Young*, Dorling Kindersley, 2006.

Thomas, David *Improving Your Memory*, Dorling Kindersley, 2003.

Trollope, Joanna *Second Honeymoon*, Bloomsbury, 2006.

Walmsley, Bernice *Teach Yourself Life at 50: For Women*, Hodder & Stoughton, 2007.

Watzlawick, Paul *The Situation Is Hopeless, but Not Serious: The Pursuit of Unhappiness*, W. W. Norton, 1993.

Whitehorn, Katherine 'Hooray! Now I Just Have Myself to Please' in the *Guardian*, 2007.

Index